EASY GUIDE TO

DEFENSIVE

SIGNALS

AT BRIDGE

EASY GUIDE TO DEFENSIVE SIGNALS AT BRIDGE

Julian Pottage

BATSFORD

First published 2005

© Julian Pottage 2005

The right of Julian Pottage to be identified as Author of this work has
been asserted by him in accordance with the Copyright, Designs and
Patents Act 1988.

ISBN 0 7134 8981 2

A CIP catalogue record for this book is available from the British Library.

Typeset in the U.K. by Ruth Edmondson
Printed in the U.K. by Creative Print & Design, Ebbw Vale,Wales

for the publishers

B T Batsford, The Chrysalis Building, Bramley Road, London W10 6SP

An imprint of **Chrysalis** Books Group plc

Distributed in the United States and Canada by Sterling Publishing Co.,
387 Park Avenue South, New York, NY 10016, USA

Editor: Elena Jeronimidis

CONTENTS

To my Godfather and Uncle, Michael Salter, who passed on from this life while the book was under preparation.

Introduction

Have you ever thought why many players, probably including yourself, find it easier to be declarer than a defender? One reason is that as declarer you can see your partner's hand while as a defender you cannot. It is so much easier to make the most of your side's assets if you can see what they are. This is where defensive signals come in. They enable the defenders to tell each other about their hands.

In the fifth edition of the *Pocket Oxford Dictionary*, the definition of a signal is *a sight or sound meant to convey orders or information*. In a bridge context *sight or sound* means the play of a card. The *orders* will tend to be a request for partner to lead or not lead a particular suit, while the *information* will tend to say something about your holding in a suit and leave partner to decide how to defend.

In bridge, people who talk about signals usually mean one of three things: an attitude signal, a count signal or a suit-preference signal. With an attitude signal you either show or deny interest in a suit. With a count signal you show whether you possess an odd or even number of cards in the suit. With a suit-preference signal you express an interest in a particular suit other than the one that you are playing. I shall of course be covering all of these in detail.

When you review the definition of signal above, it becomes clear it covers other plays. Suppose your first lead is the queen of spades. You are usually saying two or even three things about your hand: 'I have the jack of spades', 'I do not have the king of spades' and, perhaps, 'I have length in spades.' I shall deal with this type of position as well.

For any type of signal to work, at bridge or otherwise, it is necessary for three conditions to be satisfied. Firstly, the person giving the signal and the recipient must know that it is a signal. Secondly, the giver and the receiver must know what type of signal is suitable for a given moment. Thirdly, the giver needs to know how to encode the signal and the receiver to decode it. As a defender you will be the giver half the time and the receiver half the time. This means you need to start watching for your partner's signals and to play with people who will look for and act upon yours. If they are not already familiar with the content of this book, it will help you if your regular partner(s) also read it.

You will find that the signals covered in the first half of the book are simpler or, at any rate, more basic than those in the second half. If you

---

have played very few signals in the past, you may find it helpful to read the first five or six chapters several times before moving on to the second half of the book. Do not worry if there seems to be a lot to take in all at once. On many of the example deals the defenders exchange more than one signal, which means you will get frequent reminders about the earlier material. Whichever way you approach the book, you should find the effort worthwhile. Time and time again you will find that using a defensive signal transforms a 50-50 guess into a sure thing or greatly increases your chance of making the right decision.

Many people, when they first start using signals regularly, have the occasional accident. A common post-mortem goes something like this: 'Why did you signal for a club?' to which the reply comes: 'I didn't know that I had.' With practice, however, you will find that misunderstandings are few and far between and that the gains vastly outweigh the losses.

You are probably aware that there are a variety of bidding systems in use around the world (Acol, Standard American, Precision etc.). The same is true, although arguably to a more limited extent, when it comes to defensive signals. To keep life simple I have excluded discussion of the various non-standard or exclusively expert methods from the main part of the book and devoted the final chapter to this purpose.

I would very much like to thank Maureen Dennison and Peter Burrows for their usual help in weeding out errors in the original manuscript. I would also like to thank Elena Jeronimidis for suggesting the title and for her other roles in making the book happen. I must also mention Ruth Edmondson and Tony Gordon who worked on the type-setting and proof-reading respectively.

Julian Pottage
June 2005

Chapter 1
Basic Signals on Partner's Lead

If partner leads to a trick you are not trying to win, it is usual to indicate whether you like the suit with an attitude signal. A high spot card encourages (the highest you can afford) and your lowest discourages. Your holding in the suit led usually dictates your action.

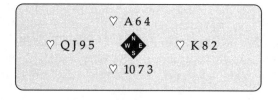

West leads the queen and declarer plays the ace from dummy. Holding the king, East should encourage with the eight – if West gets in again, the defenders have two tricks to take. This position is similar:

Again West leads the queen and dummy's ace goes up. Holding the ten, East knows West can safely continue the suit, so encourages with the seven. Remember, the lead of the queen shows Q-J, making both the king (the card above) and the ten (the card below) useful cards.

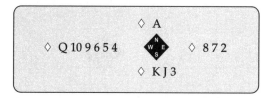

This time East has no wish to see diamonds continued. East's play of the two under the ace warns West that South has the K-J. Armed with this information, West will very likely try a different suit next time.

Everything I have said up until now applies equally to suit and no-trump contracts. However, in a suit contract, the prospect of scoring a ruff means that you may wish to encourage when holding only low cards.

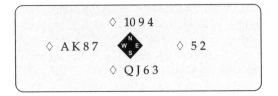

When West leads the ace (showing the king), East has hopes of a ruff. So East plays the five, and South follows with the three. West cannot be sure that the five is a high card (South might be concealing the two) but it is safe enough to continue with the king. When East plays the two next, completing a 'high-low' signal, West knows to play a third round.

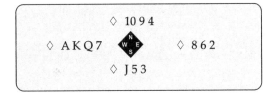

Of course, you may continue a suit despite discouragement. Here West needs no help and may continue with a second and third round (and sometimes a fourth) even though East plays the two on the first round.

The time has come to have four suits rather than one.

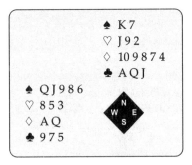

South plays in 3NT and your lead of the ♠Q loses to the king. At trick two, the ◇10 runs to your queen. What do you do next if partner's first spade was (a) the five or (b) the two?

If East played the ♠5 – a high card when you can see the six, seven, eight and nine – you will place East with the ♠10 and continue spades. If, instead, partner played the ♠2, South must have the ♠A-10. In this case, given dummy's clubs, you will try a heart in the hope East has the ♡A and three spades or ♡K-Q-10-x-(x). Even if this is not so, you avoid losing a cheap trick to the ♠10. With no signals, your play would be a guess.

I have said that usually your holding in the suit led governs whether or not to encourage. There are a few exceptions:

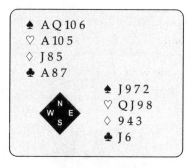

```
        ♠ A Q 10 6
        ♡ A 10 5
        ◇ J 8 5
        ♣ A 8 7
                        ♠ J 9 7 2
             N          ♡ Q J 9 8
          W     E       ◇ 9 4 3
             S          ♣ J 6
```

South opens 1♡, North bids 1♠, South rebids 2♣ and North bids 4♡ (going via fourth-suit if you like). West leads the ◇A. What do you do?

You hope partner has the ◇K (not quite as safe an assumption as usual). If your side makes the first two tricks, your trumps will set the contract. Therefore, you play the ◇9 to encourage. If you mistakenly played the ◇3, partner may switch to a spade (possibly vital if South started with ◇Q-x and two low spades). That could be a disaster if South has the singleton ♠K and discards two diamonds on the ♠A-Q.

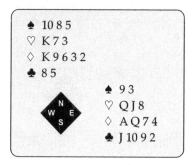

```
        ♠ 10 8 5
        ♡ K 7 3
        ◇ K 9 6 3 2
        ♣ 8 5
                        ♠ 9 3
             N          ♡ Q J 8
          W     E       ◇ A Q 7 4
             S          ♣ J 10 9 2
```

South opens 1♡ and jumps to game after North gives a simple raise. Partner leads the ♠A. Which card do you play?

Although you have a doubleton spade, any ruff would be with a natural trick and of no use. If South has the ♠Q and is void in diamonds, it could be fatal to encourage a spade continuation. Your side would make just two spades and a ruff. You should play low instead. If you were to play the nine, partner might have little choice but to continue spades. If you had ♠Q-x-x, the same hearts, but no ◇A, there could be discards coming on dummy's diamonds. You will see from the last two examples that an attitude signal says more 'please lead or do not lead this suit' rather than 'I do or do not have values in the suit.'

Attitude signals (and indeed the other signals) in this chapter apply both on the opening lead and on switches to a new suit:

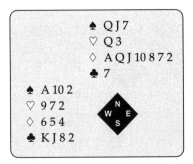

South, who has shown a fairly flat 11-12, plays in 4♠.

When you lead the ♣2, partner wins with the ace and cashes the ♡A. What do you play?

With 12 points in dummy and 8 in your hand, you know that South has the ♡K but it is possible that partner does not. Accordingly, you should play your lowest heart, the two. What you want is for partner to revert to clubs. If you can force dummy to ruff at the next trick and again when you are in with the ♠A, your ♠10 will be promoted. Admittedly, partner may not be able to work this out, but it is still worth a try. If you were not playing any signals (or if you gave the wrong signal), there would be a danger that partner would continue hearts. After all, that could be the winning move if you had the ♡K and not the ♣K.

If you really wanted, you might use attitude signals alone on partner's lead. If you do, you will be missing a wealth of opportunities. The aim of any communication is to convey information not already available. This means that, if, without a signal, partner can work out whether you like the suit, a signal should convey some other message.

West leads the ace (against a suit contract) and, assuming West would rarely lead an unsupported ace, it is clear that East can have no useful high diamonds. What West really wants to know is whether East has three diamonds, when the king will stand up, or four, when South will ruff the second round. Accordingly, East gives a count signal, playing high from an even number and low from an odd. Accepted wisdom is to play second highest from a four- or six-card suit, here the ◇4, and highest from a doubleton. To show an odd number you play your lowest card.

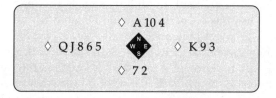

West leads the queen and dummy's ace wins. If you think about it, the position of the king is obvious. With the king in hand, declarer would capture the queen with the king, keeping the A-10 in dummy as a tenace over the jack. Therefore, here again, East should give a count signal, this time the three to denote an odd number.

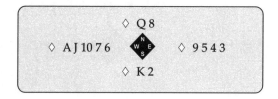

We return to no-trumps and West leads the jack, dummy playing the queen. Clearly East would put the ace or king on the queen if able so to do, thus West will know the location of all the cards down to at least the ten whatever low card East plays. What West cannot easily figure out (in the absence of a signal) is whether South's king will drop under the ace. So, East plays the five, second highest from a four-card suit.

Let us study a couple of examples with your whole hand shown:

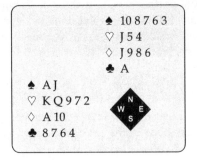

You, West, open 1♡, East bids 2♡, South overcalls with 2♠ and North raises to 4♠. Declarer wins your ♡K lead with the ace and leads the ♠K to your ace. How do you continue?

Partner would work out the ♡K was going to lose to the ace, making the heart position clear without an attitude signal. This means you read partner's first heart as count. If it was the ♡8, no doubt second highest from 10-8-6-3, desperate measures are called for. To beat the contract you will need three diamond tricks or two diamonds and a ruff, so you switch to the ◊A. If, however, it was the ♡3, low from three cards, there is no need to panic. Simply cash the ♡Q and probably exit with a heart (or a club to dummy's ace). Now you only need two diamond tricks and you should get these if partner has either the ◊K or the ◊Q.

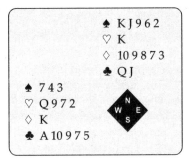

South opens 1♡, North responds 1♠ and South rebids 2◊. North raises to 3◊ and South's 3NT ends the bidding. You lead the ♣10 and dummy wins. The ◊10 runs to the king and you have the lead back.

How can you tell whether it is right to cash the ♣A (in the hope the king falls) or whether it is better to lead a low club? The latter will work better if declarer still has a club stopper and partner holds an entry.

Easy Guide to Defensive Signals at Bridge

The clue comes from partner's play in clubs. Both South's 3NT bid and East's inability to cover dummy's first club make the position of the high clubs clear. Therefore, again you can read partner's first club as a count signal. If it was the ♣6 (or the ♣4 and South played the ♣6), it cannot cost to lay down the ♣A. Partner would not dream of playing the six from 8-6-3 or 8-6-2. It must either be from 8-6-x-x or 6-x. If, instead, East played the ♣2 or ♣3, you can be sure the ♣K will not drop. In this case, you will read that very low club as indicating an odd number and try a low club. This will probably be the winning move if partner has either the ♠A or the ◊A (or possibly the ♡A).

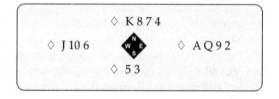

As is the case with any signal, you very rarely waste a trick in order to give a signal. When West leads the ◊J and dummy plays low, East would like to play the nine to show four cards in this side suit. This would tell West that a second trick would stand up. Unfortunately, this would be risky. After the ◊10 to the king and ace on the second round, dummy's ◊8-7 would be good for a ruffing finesse against East's queen.

So far, the leader's partner has not been in a position either to want to win the first round or to play a high card to drive out an opposing stopper. When in fact you do need to play a high card, you have less chance to signal. In this case, both attitude and count signals cease to apply. Even so, you can still do something.

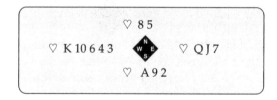

Suppose West leads the four and you have no agreement about what East should play. What happens if East plays the queen? South wins with the ace and West has no idea whether it is safe to continue the suit. Can you see why it is better for East to play the jack? If, now, South wins with the ace, West can place the queen in your hand. South, given the choice, will surely prefer to capture the jack with the queen rather than with the ace.

This position is similar. If West leads the seven and dummy plays low, East should play the ten, not the jack. When the ten forces the ace (or holds the trick) West knows who has the jack. The rule is that you play the lower of two touching honours. The play of the ♣J here, or the ♡Q in the previous example, would deny the ♣10 and ♡J respectively.

Paradoxically perhaps, when partner or the opponent in second seat is going to win the trick, you play the highest card of a sequence, just like you do on the opening lead. Of special note is the play of the queen under partner's ace. This promises a Q-J holding or a singleton queen.

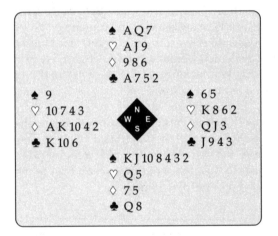

When West leads the ◇A against 4♠, East needs to drop the ◇Q. This allows West to lead a low diamond next so that East can attack clubs. If East did not play the ◇Q, West might cash a second diamond and try a club in the hope East has the ♣Q.

In deciding what constitutes a sequence, you can take account of the cards already gone or about to go. For example, if partner cashes the ace of a suit and the singleton queen is on view in dummy, you can treat K-J-10 as a sequence rather than an interior sequence and drop the king rather than jack. Needless to say, you do not jettison any high cards like this unless you think it is safe to do so.

Test Yourself

1.1 (a)

West, your partner, leads the ♠10 against 3NT. Dummy's ace goes up. Which card will you play on this trick? Might it make any difference if the contract is 4♡?

1.1 (b)

West leads the ♡Q against South's contract of 4♠. Which card will you play, and what will it signify? Might either the card or its meaning alter if you have bid hearts but partner has not supported the suit?

1.2

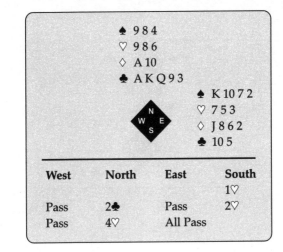

West	North	East	South
			1♡
Pass	2♣	Pass	2♡
Pass	4♡	All Pass	

Partner leads the ◊5 and dummy's ace wins. Which card do you play? What is the purpose of your play? Would you do anything different if you had J-10-7-2 of spades and K-8-6-2 of diamonds?

1.3

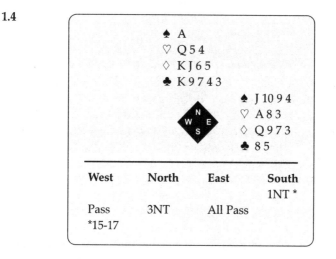

	♠ 7 4 2
	♡ —
	◊ Q 4 3
	♣ A K Q 8 6 5 3

	♠ 9 6 3
	♡ J 7
	◊ K J 9 5 2
	♣ J 10 2

West	North	East	South
			1♡
Pass	2♣	Pass	2♠
Pass	3♣	Pass	3♠
Pass	4♠	Pass	4NT
Pass	5◊	Dbl	6♠
Pass	All Pass		

What do you play when West leads the ◊A? What message will your card send?

1.4

	♠ A
	♡ Q 5 4
	◊ K J 6 5
	♣ K 9 7 4 3

	♠ J 10 9 4
	♡ A 8 3
	◊ Q 9 7 3
	♣ 8 5

West	North	East	South
			1NT *
Pass	3NT	All Pass	
*15-17			

Partner leads the ♠5 and dummy's ace wins. What card do you play?

Solutions

1.1 (a)

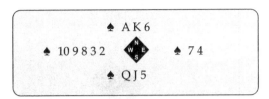

When partner leads the ♠10, your normal card is the four. Without the ♠Q, you have no reason to ask for a spade continuation. If partner leads the suit again, it will be without any expectation of finding you with strength or help in spades.

If the contract is 4♡, you might play the seven to try to get partner to give you a ruff. It largely depends upon whether you think there is a chance that your side can play a second and third round of spades before trumps are drawn. In addition, you will need a spare trump with which to ruff.

1.1 (b)

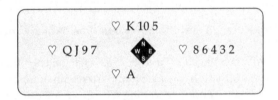

As West's lead of the ♡Q implies possession of the ♡J, you expect South to win with the ace either out of necessity (with a singleton ace) or to leave the K-10 as a tenace. Since it is clear that your hearts are all low cards, you signal length rather than attitude. Five cards is an odd number, so you play your lowest heart, the two. It may be very helpful for partner to have an idea that the ace is a singleton. In this case, declarer will have only two heart tricks rather than three and partner will know not to lead the suit again and allow a free finesse.

If you have bid hearts and partner has not supported, it does alter the situation. In this case, it is no longer clear who has the ♡J. The lead might have come from Q-x. This means that partner may well want to know who holds the ♡J. Given that you do not hold this card, you will normally wish to discourage. You play your lowest heart, the two.

You will see therefore that, although you play the same card whether or not you have bid the suit, its meaning changes.

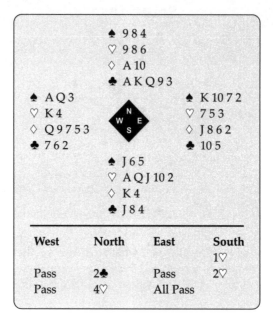

	♠ 9 8 4		
	♡ 9 8 6		
	◇ A 10		
	♣ A K Q 9 3		
♠ A Q 3		♠ K 10 7 2	
♡ K 4		♡ 7 5 3	
◇ Q 9 7 5 3		◇ J 8 6 2	
♣ 7 6 2		♣ 10 5	
	♠ J 6 5		
	♡ A Q J 10 2		
	◇ K 4		
	♣ J 8 4		

West	North	East	South
			1♡
Pass	2♣	Pass	2♡
Pass	4♡	All Pass	

Partner leads the ◇5 and dummy's ace wins. Which card do you play?

You should play the two. You do not wish to encourage a diamond continuation. Although it is true that partner can almost certainly lead a second diamond without conceding a trick, a glance at dummy tells you that safety is not the order of the day. In any case, partner can work out that it would be safe to continue diamonds. Otherwise, declarer would have played the ◇10 from dummy instead of the ace.

Look at the position from partner's point of view when, at trick two, the ♡9 runs to the king. Since it is clear that declarer will able to discard any losers on the clubs after trumps are drawn, your side will need to take the next three tricks. Assuming you have no trump trick, there are two possibilities for this. The first is to play a diamond in the hope you hold the king and can switch to a spade to pick up South's ♠K. The other chance is to switch to a spade in the hope you have the ♣K. To help partner decide what to do, you should discourage diamonds with this holding and encourage if you had ♠J-10-7-2 and ◇K-8-6-2.

You may have gathered from this discussion that if the club suit was different – say if you had the suit well stopped – you might encourage even with these jack-high diamonds. It would depend upon whether you could stand a spade switch, partner's likely alternative to playing diamonds again.

```
                    ♠ 7 4 2
                    ♡ —
                    ◊ Q 4 3
                    ♣ A K Q 8 6 5 3
   ♠ J 8                              ♠ 9 6 3
   ♡ Q 10 9 4 2         N            ♡ J 7
   ◊ A 8 7 6        W       E        ◊ K J 9 5 2
   ♣ 7 4                S            ♣ J 10 2
                    ♠ A K Q 10 5
                    ♡ A K 8 6 5 3
                    ◊ 10
                    ♣ 9
```

West	North	East	South
			1♡
Pass	2♣	Pass	2♠
Pass	3♣	Pass	3♠
Pass	4♠	Pass	4NT
Pass	5◊	Dbl	6♠
Pass	All Pass		

What do you play when West leads the ◊A? What message will your card send?

The purpose of any signal is to convey information not already clear. In other words, you do not give the same message twice. What do you think your double of 5◊ did? It announced that you had sufficient strength in diamonds to make an opening diamond lead desirable. The fact that you have the ◊K is therefore not news to partner. To double 5◊ (except as a psychic move I suppose) would be unthinkable if you had neither the ace nor the king of diamonds.

What partner cannot be so sure of is how many diamonds you hold. It might be only four, when a second diamond would stand up. Since it will not on the actual layout, partner needs to switch to a club to cut declarer off from dummy. Admittedly, if one can trust South's bidding, a second diamond will not make – North did nothing to promise a first- or second-round diamond control – and South should not use 4NT with a void (i.e. a 5-6-2-0 shape). Even so, it is better for the defenders to rely on each other rather than on the opponents. The right play is the ◊2, showing an odd number of diamonds. On the bidding partner can work out that this odd number must be five rather than three.

```
                    ♠ A
                    ♡ Q 5 4
                    ◇ K J 6 5
                    ♣ K 9 7 4 3
  ♠ K 8 6 5 3            N          ♠ J 10 9 4
  ♡ 10 9 2          W        E      ♡ A 8 3
  ◇ 8 4                  S          ◇ Q 9 7 3
  ♣ Q 10 6                          ♣ 8 5
                    ♠ Q 7 2
                    ♡ K J 7 6
                    ◇ A 10 2
                    ♣ A J 2
```

West	North	East	South
			1NT *
Pass	3NT	All Pass	
*15-17			

Partner leads the ♣5 and dummy's ace wins. What card do you play?

If you have remembered only attitude (and count) signals, you will have a problem here. If South has the ♠K, you will want partner to continue spades when the chance comes. If, instead, West has the ♠K and South the ♠Q, you will want partner not to play spades again but to put you in with the ♡A so that you can lead spades.

The solution is to drop the ♠J, denoting a sequence headed by the jack. This will leave partner well placed to decide what to do. As the cards lie, let us suppose declarer finesses the ♣J at trick two and it loses to the queen. Knowing from your play of the ♠J that South holds the ♠Q, partner will probably try the ♡10. Since the initial lead of the ♠5 can hardly be second highest from a bad suit, you will know what to do: put up the ♡A and return the ♠10. If you mistakenly played an encouraging ♠10 on the first trick, partner would probably continue with a low spade when in with the ♣Q. This would be the right thing to do if you had ♠Q-10-x-x and weaker hearts.

Note also that, in some circumstances, dropping the ♠J might avoid a spade blockage. If declarer (holding ♣A-Q-x) was able to run five club tricks and knock out your ♡A, it would be critical for your side to run four spade tricks – something that would not be possible if you had to win the fourth round of the suit.

Basic Signals on Partner's Lead in Brief

- If you are not trying to win the trick or to force out a high card, you usually give an attitude signal based on your holding in the suit led.

- To encourage, play a high spot card, the highest you can afford.

- To discourage, play your lowest card.

- You can encourage, even with no help in the suit, if you are keen to avoid a switch.

- You can discourage, even with help in the suit, if you are keen to prevent a continuation.

- The signals apply equally to a switch as to the initial lead.

- If you are not trying to win the trick or force out a high card and your strength will be clear whatever card you play, signal count.

- For a count signal, play your lowest card with an odd number in the suit and a higher card with an even number.

- For a count signal with an even number, play top of a doubleton but second highest from a four- or six-card suit.

- If you think it may cost a trick to play your normal card from an even number, signal with the highest card you can afford.

- If you are trying to win the trick or force out a high card, play the lower of touching cards.

- If you are not trying to win the trick or force out a high card, drop the highest card from a sequence.

Chapter 2
Basic Signals on
an Opponent's Lead

When declarer leads a suit from hand or dummy, you do not need to tell partner whether you want the suit led. Your opponent is already leading it. Instead, you can give a count signal, indicating an odd or an even number of cards in the suit. The rule is to play your lowest card from an odd number and a higher card from an even number. Assuming you can afford it, you play your higher card from a doubleton and your second-highest card from a four- or six-card suit.

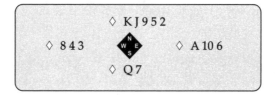

With this layout, both defenders have an odd number of diamonds and will play their lowest cards on the first round of the suit, the three and six respectively. This way both defenders can place declarer with a doubleton. This will help East to judge when to take the ace and tell West that East cannot hold a double stopper in the suit.

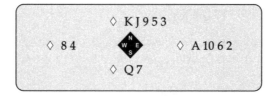

This time both defenders have an even number of diamonds and the play in the suit will be different. West plays the eight on the queen, high from a doubleton, but East cannot afford to waste the ten and plays the six. Remember the idea of giving a signal is to help you to play normal bridge and to defeat contracts, not to give tricks away. A good partner will take account of the fact that you cannot always spare a card high enough to give a clear signal.

If declarer crosses to hand with the ♠A, it will be helpful to West for East to play the nine, showing four cards in the suit. This will tell West that declarer has only three spade tricks rather than four. I say this because East would play the eight from 9-8-7-2 and, if East had only two spades, South would have four and spades would presumably be trumps. In fact, you do not give ordinary count signals in the trump suit itself.

Of course, there are times when it is unsafe to signal. It would be safe for West to play the nine in fourth seat under the king but not in second position on the five. The latter would allow declarer to finesse the seven on the next round. You must be alert to this type of layout.

A count signal has its greatest value when dummy has a long but not solid suit and no outside entry. In this case, whoever holds the stopper will wish to use it on declarer's last card to kill the suit.

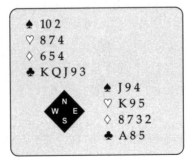

South opens 2NT and North raises to 3NT. West leads the ♠5, which goes to the ten, jack and ace. Declarer plays a club to the king and, when you play the five, continues with the queen. What do you do?

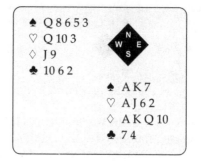

♠ Q 8 6 5 3
♡ Q 10 3
◊ J 9
♣ 10 6 2

♠ A K 7
♡ A J 6 2
◊ A K Q 10
♣ 7 4

In the absence of count signals, you would have a real problem. If these above are the two unseen hands, you had better take your ace on the second round. Two club tricks together with two spades, one heart and four diamonds would see declarer home.

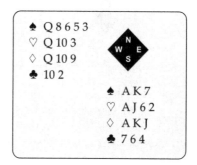

♠ Q 8 6 5 3
♡ Q 10 3
◊ Q 10 9
♣ 10 2

♠ A K 7
♡ A J 6 2
◊ A K J
♣ 7 6 4

If, alternatively, this is the layout, you need to hold up your ace for a second time. Probably you would hold up a second time because a second club trick, even if undeserved, will not necessarily see declarer home while four club tricks surely will. Luckily, you do not need to guess once you have started playing count signals.

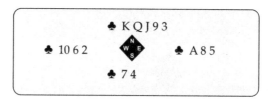

♣ K Q J 9 3

♣ 10 6 2   ♣ A 8 5

♣ 7 4

If this is the club layout, West plays the two on the first round, clearly indicating an odd number. Since, if the ♣2 is a singleton, South will have four clubs and it will not matter what you do, you should play West for three clubs and take your ace on the second round.

If this is the layout, West plays the ten on the first round. Again the ♣10 could be singleton (you need to bear in mind that partner's play may have been forced rather than a signal) but it is more likely to be top of a doubleton. One thing is sure. The ten cannot be from a three-card holding. Accordingly, you hold up your ace until the third round.

Lest you get carried away with count signals, remember that they are no substitute for normal defensive technique. When the ◊Q comes off dummy, playing the ◊3 as East 'to show an odd number' is often going to be wrong. If declarer holds A-J-10-x or, as shown here, A-J-x-x-x, you need to cover to set up a winner for partner.

Likewise, you do not want to play the ◊3 if dummy leads the two. That would allow declarer to score a cheap trick with the nine and so have no diamond loser.

In this situation, East wants to put in the queen or jack. You might wonder if the established method is to play the lower (or lowest) of touching cards with an odd number in the suit and the higher (or highest) with an even number. Somehow, that idea has never really caught on. Instead, if you want partner to know your strength, it is usually clearest to play as high as you can, although on this particular layout you could hardly play either an unsupported jack or queen.

Likewise, assuming you wish to signal, you play the top of a sequence if you are in fourth seat and are not trying to win the trick.

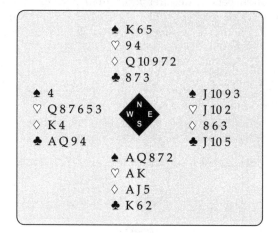

South plays in 4♠ having shown 20-22 points and a five-card spade suit. After a heart lead goes round to the ace, declarer cashes the ♠A, crosses to the ♠K and runs the ◇Q, unblocking the jack. If East has helpfully played the ♠J under the king, West will know the trump suit is not solid, and can win with the ◇K and exit passively in a red suit. If East has not done so, West may panic and, fearing that declarer has a lot of tricks ready to run, switch to a club. (Declarer could hold 20 points without the ♣K: ♠A-Q-J, ♡A-K, ◇A-J and ♣J.)

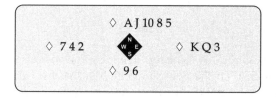

Just as you usually win with the lower of touching honours if partner leads the suit, you do the same on declarer's lead when you want partner to know your holding. If East wins the ◇9 with the queen, West will guess that East has the ◇K as well or South might have cashed it. Of course, it may be that as East you want the position to remain unclear. You might want declarer to waste an entry to hand for repeating the finesse. Alternatively you might think declarer has a choice of ways to continue. This may well be the case if this is a side suit, since a ruffing finesse would pick up your remaining holding. In those situations you play at random, playing the king half the time and the queen the other half.

I am sorry to have to include words like 'if you wish to signal' so often in this chapter. The thing is that, if the other side leads a suit, knowing its layout will often benefit declarer more than partner. As you become experienced with signals, you will get a feel for when to signal honestly. One time when there is little point in giving a signal is when you hold all the defensive strength. With few decisions to make, it can hardly help partner to know your holding. Another place for caution is in the main opposing suit. Since, as mentioned before, you do not give count in the trump suit, this advice applies mainly to no-trump contracts.

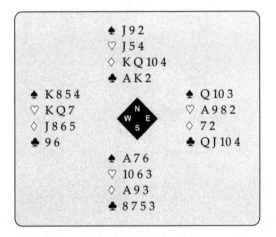

Playing Standard American (or similar), your opponents bid 1◇ – 1NT. You lead the ♠4 and are pleased to see partner win the first trick by capturing the nine with the ten. Back comes the ♠Q and declarer plays the ace this time. Now comes a low diamond. What should you do?

If partner holds the ◇A, whether you play the five or the eight will scarcely matter. With the two certain club entries on view in dummy, partner will have very little reason to hold up twice. By contrast, if South is the one with the ◇A, you need to keep stumm about your diamond holding. You do not want declarer to put up dummy's king, come back to the ◇A and finesse the ten on the third round. For the same reason East also needs to avoid habitually playing high-low in this position. If declarer knows that one of you always gives an honest signal, it is a simple matter of believing you (or your partner as the case may be) to pick up the suit whether you have J-x-x-x or x-x-x.

Another reason why you might not signal is if you cannot afford to play the 'right' card. This is especially true, as we saw on page 25, when you have a doubleton.

Perhaps you are wondering why you play your second-highest card from four or six cards. There are two answers. The first is simple. Often you cannot afford the highest. With Q-x-x-x or J-x-x-x, you would hardly want to part with your picture card – indeed there are times when your third-highest card is the best you can spare. The second is that, by playing differently with a doubleton and a longer suit, partner has the best chance of working out what you hold. After all, you do not lead high from four small cards on the opening lead, do you?

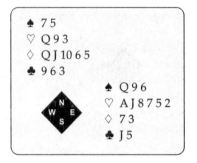

Suppose South has opened 2NT and North has raised to game. West leads the ♠4 and your queen drives out the ace. Declarer cashes the ace and king of diamonds before switching to the ♡K. West plays the ◇9, then the ◇2 and now the ♡6. Do you win this trick?

Is declarer, with ◇A-K doubleton, trying to create an entry to dummy in hearts? If so, you had better hold up your ace. Before you do, can you remember the precise diamonds partner played? They were the nine on the first round and the two on the second. If South was dealt a doubleton A-K, West had 9-8-4-2. This cannot be right: partner would have played the ◇8 on the first round, not the nine. Since declarer is unlikely to carry on with hearts and may have nine tricks if you duck the first round, you should win and return a spade. These are the other two hands:

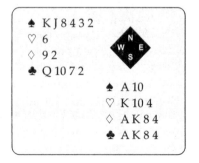

Perhaps you think that few of your regular opponents are crafty enough to conjure up the illusion of an A-K doubleton. On our final example in the main part of this chapter, you will find yourself in a hole no matter what the quality of your opposition. It also differs slightly from some of the other deals in that there is no need to consider a hold up:

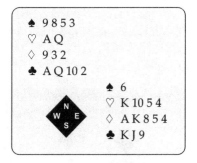

As East, you open 1♦ and hear South overcall 1♠. Your side takes no further part in the bidding and South is soon in 4♠.

Partner leads the ♦J and your side plays three rounds of the suit. South, who started with ♦Q-x, ruffs the third round high, draws two rounds of trumps and leads a club to the ten. Winning with the jack, you face an unappetising choice: lead into one of dummy's tenaces or give a ruff-and-discard. How will partner's club play affect your choice?

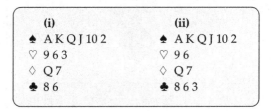

Here are a couple of typical hands for declarer. For the first, you need to return a club and wait to score a heart. For the second, you want to return a heart and await a club trick. In other words, you want to lead the suit in which South started with a doubleton. You do not know the heart layout, but partner will have given you count in clubs. If South began with two, West had four and will have played fairly high (the five from 7-5-4-3 if South has 8-6). If South began with three, West had three and will have played low, the four if South has 8-6-3. Yes, West just might have had two clubs (making South's shape 6-1-2-4), in which case you will go wrong. No method of signals is perfect, I am afraid.

Test Yourself

2.1 (a)

South, the declarer, leads the ♠10 from hand. Which card will you, West, normally play on this trick if the contract is 3NT? Would it make any difference if the contract is 4♡?

2.1 (b)

This time the lead is the ♡J from dummy. Which card will you usually play on this trick if the contract is 3NT? Would it make any difference if the contract is 4♡?

2.2

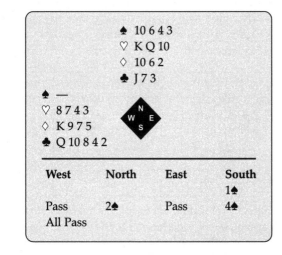

	♠ 10 6 4 3		
	♡ K Q 10		
	◇ 10 6 2		
	♣ J 7 3		

♠ —		
♡ 8 7 4 3		
◇ K 9 7 5		
♣ Q 10 8 4 2		

West	North	East	South
			1♠
Pass	2♠	Pass	4♠
All Pass			

You, West, lead the ♣4. Dummy's jack wins (ugh!) and partner plays the nine. Declarer comes to hand with the ace of spades, on which partner follows low, and leads the ♡6. What do you make of partner's ♣9 and, more importantly, what do you play now?

2.3

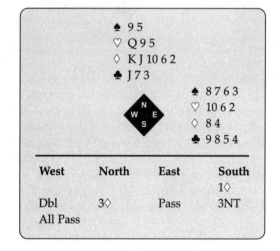

	♠ Q 10 5		
	♡ K J 6 3 2		
	◇ 7 2		
	♣ 10 5 4		

♠ A 9 7
♡ A 9 4
◇ Q 4 3
♣ Q J 3 2

West	North	East	South
			1◇
Pass	1♡	Pass	2NT*
All Pass			
*17-18			

After this old-fashioned bidding, you, West, lead the ♣2. Partner plays the king and the ace wins. Declarer lays down the ♡Q. What do you do? If you duck, partner plays the ♡8 and the ♡10 comes next. What do you do this time?

2.4

	♠ 9 5		
	♡ Q 9 5		
	◇ K J 10 6 2		
	♣ J 7 3		

♠ 8 7 6 3
♡ 10 6 2
◇ 8 4
♣ 9 8 5 4

West	North	East	South
			1◇
Dbl	3◇	Pass	3NT
All Pass			

Partner leads the ♠K and you play the three. Do you agree that this is the correct card to play? Declarer wins with the ace and crosses to the king of diamonds. Have you decided what card to play to this trick?

Solutions

2.1(a)

When declarer leads the ♠10 from hand, your normal card as West is the three. With an odd number of cards in the suit, you play your lowest card. It makes no difference to your play whether the contract is 3NT or 4♡, although it may affect what partner does with the information.

If dummy has only one entry, it might be right (in a no-trump contract) for partner to allow the ♠10 to hold to shut out dummy's suit. In a suit contract, it is more likely to be right to win the first spade with the queen rather than give declarer a fast spade trick. In any case, partner will know (even if you still have some trumps) that there is no mileage in trying to give you a spade ruff.

2.1 (b)

This time the lead is the ♡J from dummy and now you have an even number of cards in the suit. With a doubleton, the normal card to play is the higher, the eight. Although with the length in the closed hand it is less likely that a hold up will kill the hearts, there will often be a benefit for West in saving the ace for later. For one thing, declarer will need to use a side entry to run the suit. For another, knowing that you will show out on the third round, partner might wish to wait for you to make a revealing discard. Also, if South holds ♡A-K-10-x-x, then West, after scoring the ♡Q, may be able to count declarer for four heart tricks.

This time it would a make a difference if the contract is 4♡. In this case, hearts are trumps. You do not play high-low in the trump suit to signal a doubleton and so would play the four first. (You will find out in Chapter 8 what a high-low in trumps does signify.)

2.2

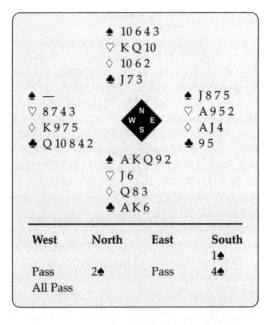

	♠ 10 6 4 3	
	♡ K Q 10	
	◇ 10 6 2	
	♣ J 7 3	
♠ —		♠ J 8 7 5
♡ 8 7 4 3		♡ A 9 5 2
◇ K 9 7 5		◇ A J 4
♣ Q 10 8 4 2		♣ 9 5
	♠ A K Q 9 2	
	♡ J 6	
	◇ Q 8 3	
	♣ A K 6	

West	North	East	South
			1♠
Pass	2♠	Pass	4♠
All Pass			

You, West, make the unfortunate lead of the ♣4. Dummy's jack wins and partner plays the nine. In this situation, partner's inability to beat the ♣J makes the location of the high clubs clear to you. Therefore, this was a count situation on the first trick and the ♣9 (unless it was singleton of course) looks like the top of a doubleton.

Declarer comes to hand with the ace of spades, on which partner follows low, and leads the ♡6. This again is a count situation. Partner may have the ♡A and need to play it on the same trick as South's last heart. With an even number of hearts, you will not play your lowest heart. The right card to play from four low cards is your second-highest card, in this case the seven. After you play the ♡7 and dummy's king goes up, partner is sure that declarer has another heart left and ducks. Although declarer may take the marked finesse against the ♠J and draw the missing trumps, you should defeat the contract if you are careful. Since your low hearts are a liability rather than asset, you will throw those away and keep at least one long club. In any event, it does not matter whether you can picture the end result. The key thing is to make sure that partner has a true count on the hearts and does not mistakenly place declarer with a singleton.

```
                    ♠ Q 10 5
                    ♡ K J 6 3 2
                    ◇ 7 2
                    ♣ 10 5 4
      ♠ A 9 7                       ♠ J 8 4
      ♡ A 9 4          N            ♡ 8 5
      ◇ Q 4 3      W       E        ◇ 10 8 6 5
      ♣ Q J 3 2        S            ♣ K 8 7 6
                    ♠ K 6 3 2
                    ♡ Q 10 7
                    ◇ A K J 9
                    ♣ A 9
```

West	North	East	South
			1◇
Pass	1♡	Pass	2NT*
All Pass			
*17-18			

You, West, lead the ♣2. Partner plays the king and the ace wins. Declarer lays down the ♡Q and it looks right to duck. For one thing, it seems unlikely that the ♡Q is a singleton. For another, even if it is, it may still work best to hold up. Partner plays the ♡8 on the first round of hearts and declarer next leads the ♡10. What do you do this time?

The key to deciding what to do hinges on how you place the missing hearts. The two hearts you have not yet seen are the seven and the five. If South has neither card, you will place partner with an original holding of 8-7-5. However, nobody would play the eight first with that holding. Accordingly, you place declarer with an original three-card holding and hold up once more. Indeed, even if South had led the seven on the second round, you could still work out the position. Partner would not play the eight first from 10-8-5.

After taking the ♡A on the third round, you cash the ♣Q-J and play a fourth round. Partner will win and lead a diamond up to the weakness in dummy. After winning this, declarer has a 50% chance of going down. Playing a spade to the queen will work but finessing the ten will not. A 50% chance is better than none at all, which would be the case if you let your opponent score four easy heart tricks.

2.4

```
                    ♠ 9 5
                    ♡ Q 9 5
                    ◇ K J 10 6 2
                    ♣ J 7 3
   ♠ K Q J 4                        ♠ 8 7 6 3
   ♡ A 8 7 3          N             ♡ 10 6 2
   ◇ Q 3          W       E         ◇ 8 4
   ♣ Q 10 2           S             ♣ 9 8 5 4
                    ♠ A 10 2
                    ♡ K J 4
                    ◇ A 9 7 5
                    ♣ A K 6
```

West	North	East	South
			1◇
Dbl	3◇	Pass	3NT
All Pass			

Partner leads the ♠K and you play the three. Firstly, do you agree that this is the correct card to play? Since the lead of the king promises the queen but does not promise the jack, and the jack is not on view in dummy, you should express attitude based on whether you hold the jack. Without this card, you correctly play a discouraging three. As the cards lie partner would find a count signal more helpful, but you cannot vary your methods from deal to deal depending upon what you hold.

After winning with the ♠A, declarer crosses to the ◇K. Have you decided what card to play to this trick?

As a rule, with a weak hand you try to help partner by giving what signals you can. All the same, you should be wary of revealing your holding in a suit that declarer is intent on playing. Partner will find out the position when you show out on the third round whatever you do. Can you see the danger of making an automatic high-low signal? The declarer may abandon any plans for finessing against your possible ◇Q (remember: a player who makes a take-out double often has a singleton in the suit opened) and will play for the drop. On this type of layout the information that you have a doubleton diamond is of far more use to your opponent than to partner.

Basic Signals on an Opponent's Lead in Brief

- If you wish to signal, play your lowest card with an odd number and a higher card with an even number in the suit.

- With an even number, play top of a doubleton but second highest from a four- or six-card suit.

- If you think it may cost a trick to play your normal card from an even number, signal with the highest card you can afford.

- Beware of showing your length in a suit if doing so may save declarer from a decision whether to finesse or play for the drop.

- If you need to play an honour, for example to cover an honour or to prevent declarer from winning a trick cheaply, this can take precedence over giving a count signal.

- Pay close attention to the cards partner plays. If by any chance you missed the first one and the second is the two, you can be sure partner played a higher one first and is playing high-low.

- You do not signal attitude in a suit declarer or dummy leads.

- You can drop an honour in fourth seat to indicate a sequence headed by that honour.

- If you play from an honour sequence in second seat and want partner to know your holding, again play high.

Chapter 3
Basic Discards

Whenever you run out of a suit and do not intend to ruff, you will need to discard. Usually you will wish to send a message as you do so, suggesting what suit you would like led. The same principle as when following to partner's lead applies: a high-spot card expresses interest in the suit discarded, while a low card denies it. Since you often cannot spare any cards in the suit you want led, it is more common to discard a low card (your lowest card) in a suit you do not want led than a high card (the highest spot card you can afford) in a suit you do.

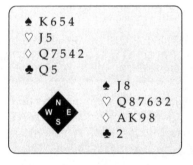

After you have bid hearts, South, who has shown a decent club suit, plays in 3NT. Partner leads the ♡9, dummy and you play low and the ace wins. Declarer leads a club to the ♣Q, on which West plays the ♣J, and leads a second club.

You would like to discard the ◊9 but can ill afford to do so. You may need four diamond tricks and a club to defeat the contract. Perhaps partner will work out that you do not like hearts from your ♡2 at trick one. Unfortunately, some people would take more notice of the fact that the ♡9 apparently forced out the ace. To confirm the message that you do not want hearts, discard the ♡3. If your hearts were good, (a) you could afford a higher one than the three and (b) you might not be throwing a heart at all. As it happens, declarer ducks this second round of clubs so that you cannot make a second discard. You will be pleased to hear that your signal gets through: West switches to the ◊J (from J-10-x) and you beat the contract with four diamonds and a club.

```
                    ♠ K 3
                    ♡ A K 7
                    ◇ A Q J 9 6 5
                    ♣ 9 4
                                    ♠ 7 6 2
                    N               ♡ 9 5 4 2
                W       E           ◇ K 7 2
                    S               ♣ K 7 2
```

West	North	East	South
	1◇	Pass	1NT
Pass	3NT	All Pass	

West leads the ♠Q (standard leads) and the king wins. Declarer comes to hand with the ♡Q and runs the ◇10. What should you do?

Many players would simply take the first diamond and return a spade. This will work fine if West has the first of the two hands below:

(i)	(ii)
♠ A Q J 9 5	♠ Q J 9 8 5
♡ J 8 3	♡ J 8 3
◇ 4	◇ 4
♣ J 10 6 5	♣ A J 10 5

Your side will make one diamond trick and four spades to defeat the contract by one. Alas, you do not fare well if partner has the second hand. Facing this, you need to switch to a low club. This will let partner win cheaply, put you back in the ♣K, and score two more club tricks even though South started with ♣Q-x-x-x.

At this stage you cannot tell whether to play for case (i) or (ii). To find out, you should hold up in diamonds. Now partner can discard on the second round, with luck something more revealing than a nondescript heart. An encouraging discard will not be safe but a low card from one black suit will tell you to try your luck in the other. Given that both defenders can count declarer for at least nine tricks, three hearts, five diamonds and the ♠K, the need to give a clear signal is apparent. (You will find out when we revisit discards in Chapter 9 that you would also have an idea of what to do if partner discarded a heart.)

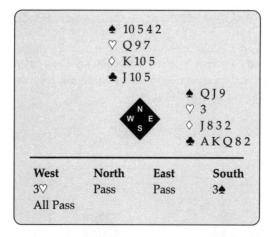

	♠ 10 5 4 2		
	♡ Q 9 7		
	◊ K 10 5		
	♣ J 10 5		

♠ Q J 9
♡ 3
◊ J 8 3 2
♣ A K Q 8 2

West	North	East	South
3♡	Pass	Pass	3♠
All Pass			

Partner, who is vulnerable, cashes the ♡A and continues with the ♡K. What do you discard?

One possible way to get partner to lead a club next is to discard an encouraging ♣8. Another is to throw a discouraging ◊2. Sadly, neither tactic is likely to work. Unless you do something spectacular, partner will continue with a third round of hearts to allow you to ruff.

With this hand you do not want to ruff. You will make a spade trick in any event. What you would hate to happen is to score your trump trick on the third round of hearts while South discards a club.

You may remember that in following either to partner's or an opposing lead you might play a very high card to denote a sequence headed by that card. The same applies with a discard. If you throw the ♣A, even the most unobservant partner will sit up and take notice. Although it is true this might cost a second undertrick (if West's shape is 0-7-4-2), that is of little consequence.

	◊ 10 2	
◊ 9 3		◊ Q J 8 7 6
	◊ A K 5 4	

In deciding what constitutes a sequence, you can take account of cards already played. After the ◊9 goes to the ten, jack and ace, the queen, eight and seven are all equals and East might discard the ◊Q.

Sometimes, indeed quite often, declarer runs a long suit in the hope that the defenders throw the wrong things. On some hands, it is clear what you need to keep. On others, however, what one defender needs to keep in a suit depends on what help the other defender can offer. The solution can be to use an attitude signal not actually to ask for a suit but merely to indicate that you can protect it.

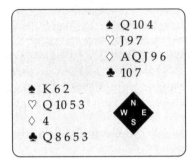

```
                          ♠ Q 10 4
                          ♡ J 9 7
                          ◊ A Q J 9 6
                          ♣ 10 7
        ♠ K 6 2
        ♡ Q 10 5 3            N
        ◊ 4                W     E
        ♣ Q 8 6 5 3            S
```

South opens a strong 1NT and North raises to 3NT. You lead the ♣5, East plays the ♣A and South the ♣J. Back comes the ♣2 and the king wins on your right. Declarer, who has five diamonds as well as dummy, proceeds to run the suit.

```
        (i)                    (ii)
   ♠ A 9 5 3              ♠ J 9 5 3
   ♡ 8 6 2                ♡ K 8 2
   ◊ 7 5                  ◊ 7 5
   ♣ A 9 4 2              ♣ A 9 4 2
```

After you have discarded a spade and a heart, life becomes a bit more difficult. If partner has a hand like (i) above, you need to keep all your three remaining hearts, and can spare a spade and a club or even two more spades. If, instead, partner has a hand like (ii), you need to keep both your remaining spades but can afford to bare your ♡Q.

The key is to watch what partner discards. With hand (i), it will be an easy decision to discard the ♠9, telling you not to worry about spades. With hand (ii), it is less clear-cut. Unless you are playing match-point pairs, partner may well discard a low spade on the basis that there is no hope if South has ♠A-K-x-x. Alternatively, partner with hand (ii) will discard either a club or the ♡8. So it boils down to this: if you see an encouraging spade, you will keep hearts. If not, you keep spades.

No matter what system of discards you play, you will not have the perfect card to throw on every deal. On occasion, you need to rely on a negative or subtle inference. That is life. Actually there are times when you cannot give any sort of signal:

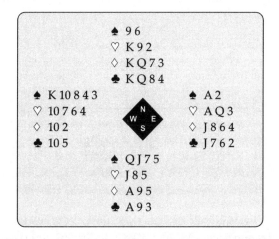

South plays in 3NT after the simple auction 1NT(12-14) – 3NT. West leads the ♠4 and the ace wins. You return the ♠2 and West captures the ♠Q with the king before leading the eight.

Clearly, whatever it means, you need to discard the ♡3 on the third round of spades. You need to keep four cards in each minor to stop dummy from scoring a long card and it would be daft to discard the ♡Q. Actually, since you know West is unlikely to regain the lead, your inability to signal is not an issue. Even if that were not the case, the need to keep a vital winner always takes precedence over giving any sort of signal. As the cards lie, it would be fatal to weaken your holding in either minor. Declarer would cash four rounds of that suit and put you in with the fourth round of the other minor to force you to lead up to the ♡K. This line would not be too difficult to find because there would be no hope of making the contract if West, who has two winning spades left, held the ♡A.

You need to bear this sort of situation in mind when you are trying to work out what partner's discard means. Fortunately, as we shall see when we return to the subject of discards in Chapter 9, this is not the end of the story. If you wish to use them, there are some more tools at your disposal to send a message with a discard.

Test Yourself

3.1

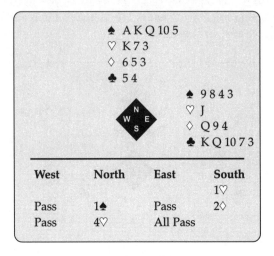

		♠ A K Q 10 5	
		♡ K 7 3	
		◇ 6 5 3	
		♣ 5 4	

			♠ 9 8 4 3
			♡ J
			◇ Q 9 4
			♣ K Q 10 7 3

West	North	East	South
			1♡
Pass	1♠	Pass	2◇
Pass	4♡	All Pass	

Partner leads the ♣2 and you play the queen, the lower of touching cards, and the ace wins. Declarer crosses to the ♡K and plays a second round of trumps. What should you discard?

3.2

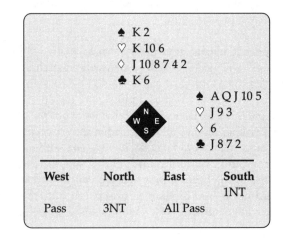

		♠ K 2	
		♡ K 10 6	
		◇ J 10 8 7 4 2	
		♣ K 6	

			♠ A Q J 10 5
			♡ J 9 3
			◇ 6
			♣ J 8 7 2

West	North	East	South
			1NT
Pass	3NT	All Pass	

After this strong no-trump sequence, West leads the ♡4. You cover the ten with the jack and the ace wins. Declarer now leads the ◇K. Do you want partner to win this? Let us say the ◇K holds and the ◇Q comes next. What do you discard when partner take this with the ◇A?

3.3

```
              ♠ 9 8 3
              ♡ A J
              ◇ 9 7 6 3 2
              ♣ J 10 9
♠ 6
♡ Q 10 7 3          N
◇ A K J 10 8    W       E
♣ A 6 2              S
```

West	North	East	South
1◇	Pass	Pass	Dbl
1♡	Pass	2♡	2♠
Pass	3♠	Pass	4♠
All Pass			

You, West, lead the ◇A. All follow and, when you continue with the ◇K, partner discards the ♡2. You continue with the ◇J, East discards the ♡4 and South ruffs. Next come three rounds of trumps. Partner follows low while you discard a heart and a diamond. Now declarer leads the ♡5. What do you think of the play so far, and what do you do now?

3.4

```
              ♠ K Q J 9 4 3
              ♡ K 6 2
              ◇ 9 2
              ♣ 9 6
♠ 8 2
♡ Q J 7             N
◇ K 10 8 7 6 5  W       E
♣ A 5               S
```

West	North	East	South
			1♣
1◇	1♠	Pass	1NT*
Pass	3NT	All Pass	
*15-17			

You lead the ◇7 and partner's jack loses to the queen. Declarer cashes the ♠A, crosses to the ♠K and discards a club on the third round of spades. What should you discard?

Solutions

3.1

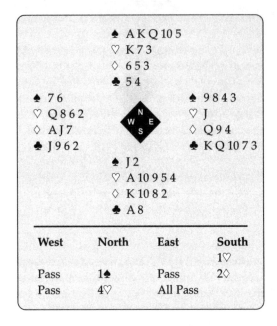

	♠ A K Q 10 5	
	♡ K 7 3	
	◇ 6 5 3	
	♣ 5 4	

♠ 7 6		♠ 9 8 4 3
♡ Q 8 6 2		♡ J
◇ A J 7		◇ Q 9 4
♣ J 9 6 2		♣ K Q 10 7 3

	♠ J 2	
	♡ A 10 9 5 4	
	◇ K 10 8 2	
	♣ A 8	

West	North	East	South
			1♡
Pass	1♠	Pass	2◇
Pass	4♡	All Pass	

Partner leads the ♣2 and you play the queen, the lower of touching cards, and the ace wins. Declarer crosses to the ♡K and plays a second round of trumps. What should you discard?

The most important information you want to convey is that you hold the ♣K. Accordingly, you should discard the ♣10. Your play of the ♣Q did not show the ♣K. It merely left open the possibility.

Most likely, declarer will insert the ♡10 on the second round, allowing the queen to win. West, having seen your discard, will continue with a club to your king, after which your diamond switch will sink the contract.

Possibly, you would achieve the same result by discarding the ◇4. The risk, however, is that the ◇4 might be an encouraging card from K-4-2. When it is safe to do so, it is better to discard an unambiguous high card that partner is sure to notice.

If you fail to make it clear that you hold the ♣K, partner might switch to the ◇7 in the hope you held the ◇K. If you had the ◇K and not the ♣K, you could then beat the contract with three diamonds and a heart.

3.2

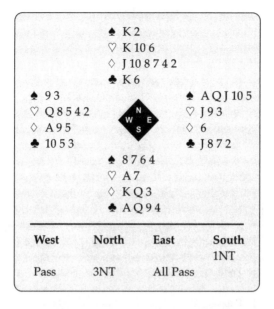

	♠ K 2		
	♡ K 10 6		
	◊ J 10 8 7 4 2		
	♣ K 6		

```
              ♠ K 2
              ♡ K 10 6
              ◊ J 10 8 7 4 2
              ♣ K 6
♠ 9 3                        ♠ A Q J 10 5
♡ Q 8 5 4 2      N           ♡ J 9 3
◊ A 9 5       W     E        ◊ 6
♣ 10 5 3         S           ♣ J 8 7 2
              ♠ 8 7 6 4
              ♡ A 7
              ◊ K Q 3
              ♣ A Q 9 4
```

West	North	East	South
			1NT
Pass	3NT	All Pass	

After this strong no-trump sequence, West leads the ♡4. You cover the ten with the jack and the ace wins. Declarer now leads the ◊K. Do you want partner to win this trick?

Although you do want partner to have a diamond stopper, you would prefer not to see it played yet. You want to make a discard first. Let us say the ◊K holds and the ◊Q comes next. What do you discard when partner take this with the ◊A?

The clear discard is the ♠Q, which will almost certainly goad partner into trying a spade next. The main snag is that South might hold four spades. In this case, you would only be able to take three spade tricks – not enough to beat the contract. The other snag is that you will be giving up a second undertrick if South has three spades. The right card is the ♣2. If you do not want clubs, partner should be able to work out you do want spades. After all, a heart cannot do much good when both of you can count declarer for nine tricks: five diamonds, two hearts and ace-king in one of the black suits. You need not worry about the fact that your club discard weakens your stopper in the suit. You expect to make the next five tricks if you can persuade partner to lead a spade.

You may wish to note that West took the ◊A on the second round in case declarer had five running club tricks. If, however, West held up twice, you could make two discards. That would allow you to discard the ♡3 and the ♣2 to discourage both those suits.

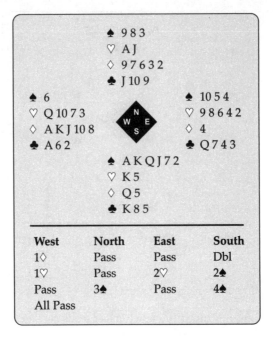

West	North	East	South
1◇	Pass	Pass	Dbl
1♡	Pass	2♡	2♠
Pass	3♣	Pass	4♠
All Pass			

You, West, lead the ◇A. All follow and, when you continue with the ◇K, partner discards the ♡2. You continue with the ◇J, East discards the ♡4 and South ruffs. Next come three rounds of trumps. Partner follows low while you discard a heart and a diamond. Now declarer leads the ♡5. What do you think of the play so far, and what do you do now?

You did the right thing continuing diamonds. With dummy short of entries, you wanted to give nothing away. Moreover, East's ♡2 discard told you there was no point in leading a heart. It was also right to lead the ◇J at the third trick, the one card that told partner there was no need to ruff. (We will examine continuations in more detail in Chapter 5). It was also fine to discard the ◇8 and one of your low hearts. Since it looks like clubs is the key suit on the deal, you want to preserve your holding there. This brings us back to your play on the ♡5.

If partner does not hold the ♡K (remember the ♡2 discard) you will need two club tricks to beat the contract. All will be well if East has the ♣K and South the ♣Q. You can also do it with the ♣Q and the ♣K the other way round. The trick is to stop declarer from taking two club finesses. To make sure that a finesse of the ♡J will not provide an entry you rise with the ♡Q. Then when you take the ♣A you will exit safely with the ◇10 or a heart and declarer will have to play clubs from hand.

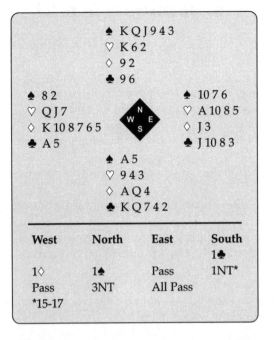

West	North	East	South
			1♣
1◊	1♠	Pass	1NT*
Pass	3NT	All Pass	
*15-17			

You lead the ◊7 and partner's jack loses to the queen. Declarer cashes the ♠A, crosses to the ♠K and discards a club on the third round of spades. What should you discard?

If you ignore the issue of giving a signal, you might feel inclined to discard the ♣5. This is most unlikely to cost a trick. Unfortunately, it will not help partner very much. What is more, with a running six-card suit in dummy, you need to think in terms of a discard strategy rather than a single discard. Since declarer still has the ◊A and you are never going to be able to hang to all your diamonds, it makes sense to discard an informative card in the suit. Can you see what that is?

With the ◊J and ◊Q gone and the ◊9 sure to fall on the next round your K-10-8 constitute a sequence. You should therefore discard the ◊K. This tells partner that your diamonds are solid apart from the ace and, as you bid, that you have values elsewhere. In any case, partner will need to place you with the ♣A because a second minor-suit ace to go with the ◊Q and six spades would be declarer's ninth trick.

If you fail to convey the message that the diamonds are not running, partner may well discard the ♡10 on the fourth round of spades. Then it will no longer be possible to make the four heart tricks that your side needs to defeat the contract.

Basic Discards in Brief

- Normally you throw losers and keep winners, just as if you are not playing any discard system.

- If you wish to signal when making a discard, the size of the card indicates whether or not you want the suit led.

- To ask for the suit discarded, throw a high-spot card.

- To discourage the suit you discard, throw your lowest card.

- You can either discourage or encourage a suit already played.

- If you have a stopper in trumps or the main opposing suit, it can be a good idea to hold it up until partner can discard.

- If it is clear what partner will lead when next in, you can signal strength in a suit you do not actually want led to make it easy for partner to know what to keep.

- If you can only spare one or two cards in your hand, the need to play safe takes precedence over giving a signal.

- If you have a sequence and wish to signal it to partner, discard your highest card in the suit.

- If partner will win the trick on which you make your discard and the right next lead will defeat the contract, you need not worry about unguarding a suit.

- If you have the chance to make two discards, you might throw discouraging cards in two suits to direct partner's attention to a third suit.

- Pay attention to partner's discards, especially the first one.

Chapter 4
Basic Suit-preference Signals

A suit-preference signal is unlike the signals you have seen so far. With this type of signal you do not ask for the suit you play. Indeed, you most commonly give a suit-preference signal in a suit you know that partner cannot play. The classic situation is when delivering a ruff. Suppose that diamonds are trumps and partner can ruff spades. In this case, you will want to tell partner whether to play a club or a heart after ruffing a spade. Since hearts is the higher-ranking suit, the thing to do is to lead a high spade if you want a heart. You lead a low spade if you want to ask for the lower-ranking club suit.

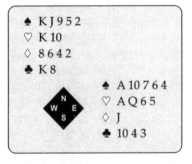

```
        ♠ K J 9 5 2
        ♡ K 10
        ◇ 8 6 4 2
        ♣ K 8
                      ♠ A 10 7 6 4
              N       ♡ A Q 6 5
           W     E    ◇ J
              S       ♣ 10 4 3
```

South opens 1◇ and rebids 2◇ over North's 1♠ response. North's raise to 3◇ ends the bidding and partner leads the ♠Q.

The ♠Q, in a suit bid by dummy, is surely a singleton. This being the case you want to capture the king with the ace and return a spade for partner to ruff. The more difficult part of the equation, at least before you read the introductory paragraph, is getting partner to lead a heart back. This should enable you to score two tricks with your ace and queen. Then you might play a third round of spades to promote a trump trick if West started with ◇K-x or ◇Q-x-x.

With values in the higher non-trump suit, hearts, you should play back your highest spade, the ten. If this does not get the message across, nothing will. Of course, if you had A-Q-x-x of clubs and rubbish in hearts you would return your lowest spade, the four.

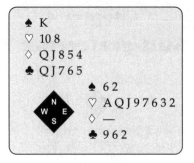

You open 4♡ and South's overcall of 4♠ ends the auction. Partner leads the ♡4 and South plays the five under your ace.

You do not need to have strength in a suit that you want led for a suit-preference signal. The ability to ruff is just as good. Clearly, you want partner to lead a diamond after ruffing South's heart king. Excluding trumps, spades, and the suit partner is ruffing, hearts, diamonds is the higher-ranking of the remaining suits. Therefore, you return the ♡Q. If, instead, your void were in clubs, you would return the ♡2.

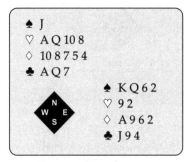

You are not always so lucky as to hold an ace or a void. Luckily, a king may do. Here South is in 4♡ having opened a weak 1NT and shown a four-card heart suit in reply to Stayman. Partner leads the ◊3.

It seems a safe bet that the lead is a singleton, which means you can count on a diamond ruff as well as your ace. Partner, you hope, has the ♠A, which will give you a third trick. It will also, if you think about it, give the means for a fourth. To tell partner that it is safe to underlead the ♠A, you return your highest diamond, the nine. A second ruff will then sink the contract. What would you do if you had the ♣K rather than the ♠K? In this case, you would return your lowest diamond, clubs obviously being lower ranking than spades.

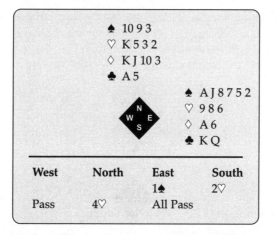

	♠ 10 9 3		
	♡ K 5 3 2		
	◊ K J 10 3		
	♣ A 5		

		♠ A J 8 7 5 2
		♡ 9 8 6
		◊ A 6
		♣ K Q

West	North	East	South
		1♠	2♡
Pass	4♡	All Pass	

Partner leads the ♣4 and South follows with the ♣6 under your ace. What is your plan for four tricks?

It is tempting to think along the following lines: 'I shall give partner a spade ruff and ask for a diamond return by leading back a high spade. This way I shall regain the lead quickly and give partner a second ruff.'

Can you see the flaw in this analysis? There are four trumps in dummy, three in your hand and South, who overcalled in hearts, must have at least five. This means that partner has at most a singleton trump and will not be able to ruff the third round of spades. There is then a real danger, particularly if partner does not hold the ◊Q, that declarer will have ten tricks: five hearts, one spade, three diamonds and a club.

You cannot fault partner for obeying your instructions. If declarer had two losing diamonds (A-Q in your hand) and a singleton king of clubs, it could be essential to play a diamond through the king.

You need to aim for a different four tricks: one spade, one ruff and one trick in each minor. At trick two, return the ♠2, your lowest spade, to ask for the lower-ranking minor, clubs. Again, partner ruffs and leads the suit for which you asked, this time with more success.

You will see from this, albeit slightly exceptional, example that you do not necessarily have a quick entry in the suit you ask partner to lead. As the name suggests, a suit-preference signal indicates a *preference* between suits rather than a *guarantee* of any particular holding.

A similar situation to leading a suit that partner can ruff is when you lead a suit in which you think partner has a singleton. Again, you know that partner cannot return the suit and will want to know which other suit to lead. On our next example you are the defender wanting a ruff:

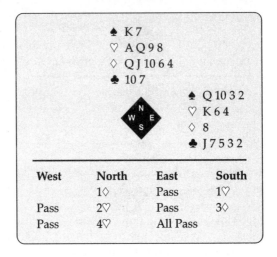

	♠ K 7		
	♡ A Q 9 8		
	♢ Q J 10 6 4		
	♣ 10 7		

	♠ Q 10 3 2
	♡ K 6 4
	♢ 8
	♣ J 7 5 3 2

West	North	East	South
	1♢	Pass	1♡
Pass	2♡	Pass	3♢
Pass	4♡	All Pass	

Partner leads the ♣A, on which you play the two, and switches to the ♢9. Declarer wins in hand with the ace and runs the ♡J to your king.

Without suit-preference signals, you would return a club in the hope partner wins with the king and leads a diamond for you to ruff. After all, at the four level and below, the initial lead of an ace implies the king to support it. Of course, West may not have the ♣K. With unsupported aces in both unbid suits, West would have to lead something.

The key here is the size of the diamond partner led. Given that South had supported diamonds, partner presumably led a diamond in the hope of setting up a ruff. Therefore, you read the ♢9, clearly a high card, as suit-preference for spades and return a spade, playing partner for a hand like (i) below. With one like (ii), West would have switched to the ♢2, a low card to ask for the lower-ranking club suit.

(i)	(ii)
♠ A 9 6 4	♠ J 9 6 4
♡ 7 5	♡ 7 5
♢ 9 5 2	♢ 9 5 2
♣ A 9 6 4	♣ A K 6 4

You have seen from that example that you can give a suit-preference signal on a trick that you expect declarer to win. The reason is that, when West led a diamond, it was likely East would be unable to return the suit. An extension to this is to use a suit-preference signal when you are setting up winners in your hand and want to tell partner how to reach them. This can happen in a no-trump contract. You will recall that you exclude the trump suit from the suits for which you can signal. Although you cannot do that in a no-trump contract, there is usually one suit you cannot reasonably want – dummy's long suit, for example.

```
                    ♠ J 9
                    ♡ Q 8 3
                    ◇ A K 9 8 4
                    ♣ Q 8 4
        ♠ K 10 8 5 2         ♠ A 6
        ♡ 7 4              N        ♡ 9 6 5 2
        ◇ 10 6 5       W       E    ◇ Q 7 3
        ♣ A 10 7           S        ♣ 9 6 5 2
                    ♠ Q 7 4 3
                    ♡ A K J 10
                    ◇ J 2
                    ♣ K J 3
```

South plays in 3NT on the simple auction 1NT(15-17) – 3NT. You lead the ♠5 and the ace beats dummy's nine. East returns the ♠6 and South, who played the ♠3 on the first round, covers with the ♠7.

The spade position does not seem entirely clear. East might have started with either A-6-4 or A-6 doubleton. (We will discuss returns in detail in the next chapter). Fortunately, since you have a sure entry, you can cater for both possibilities. If you win with the ♠K, your 10-8 will be equals against South's queen.

In this situation, in which either the ♠10 or the ♠8 would do the job of knocking out declarer's stopper, you should make a suit-preference signal. The strong diamonds in dummy make it clear that you cannot want a diamond back – indeed partner is going to get in with the ◇Q when declarer runs the ◇J. You therefore need to express preference between hearts and clubs. Holding the ace in the lower-ranking club suit you should lead the ♠8. If you had the ♡A rather than ♣A, you would lead the ♠10 instead. True, the ♠2 would be a clearer low card, but you cannot afford to lead that low when South has ♠Q-4 left.

4.1

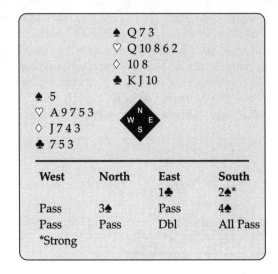

	♠ Q 7 3		
	♡ Q 10 8 6 2		
	◇ 10 8		
	♣ K J 10		

♠ 5
♡ A 9 7 5 3
◇ J 7 4 3
♣ 7 5 3

West	North	East	South
		1♣	2♠*
Pass	3♠	Pass	4♠
Pass	Pass	Dbl	All Pass
*Strong			

Reading partner's double as lead-directing, you lay down the ♡A. This wins the first trick when East discards the ◇A! How do you continue?

4.2

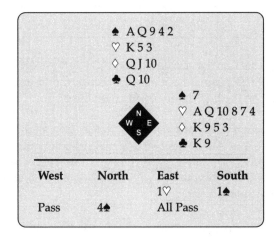

♠ A Q 9 4 2
♡ K 5 3
◇ Q J 10
♣ Q 10

♠ 7
♡ A Q 10 8 7 4
◇ K 9 5 3
♣ K 9

West	North	East	South
		1♡	1♠
Pass	4♠	All Pass	

After this sequence from the rubber bridge table, West leads the ♡J. You overtake with the ♡Q and cash the ♡A, on which West discards a low club. How do you continue?

4.3

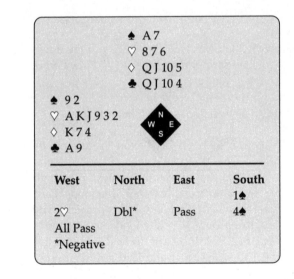

	♠ K 10 9 6		
	♡ 9		
	◇ K J 7 4 3		
	♣ K 10 4		

			♠ A 2
			♡ J 8 7 3 2
			◇ A 10 8 6 5
			♣ 7

West	North	East	South
			1NT[1]
Pass	2♣	Pass	2♠[2]
Pass	4♠	All Pass	

[1]15-17
[2]Four spades and not four hearts

Partner leads the ◇9 and dummy plays low. What is your plan for four defensive tricks?

4.4

	♠ A 7		
	♡ 8 7 6		
	◇ Q J 10 5		
	♣ Q J 10 4		

♠ 9 2			
♡ A K J 9 3 2			
◇ K 7 4			
♣ A 9			

West	North	East	South
			1♠
2♡	Dbl*	Pass	4♠
All Pass			

*Negative

You lead the ♡A, on which East plays the four and South the five. What are partner's possible heart holdings and how should you continue? Would it make any difference if South had played the ten?

Solutions

4.1

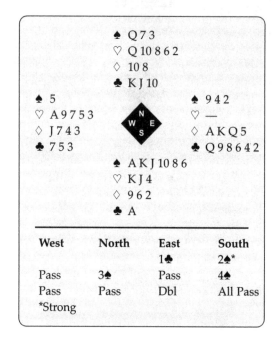

	♠ Q 7 3	
	♡ Q 10 8 6 2	
	◇ 10 8	
	♣ K J 10	
♠ 5		♠ 9 4 2
♡ A 9 7 5 3		♡ —
◇ J 7 4 3		◇ A K Q 5
♣ 7 5 3		♣ Q 9 8 6 4 2
	♠ A K J 10 8 6	
	♡ K J 4	
	◇ 9 6 2	
	♣ A	

West	North	East	South
		1♣	2♠*
Pass	3♠	Pass	4♠
Pass	Pass	Dbl	All Pass
*Strong			

Reading partner's double as lead-directing, you lay down the ♡A. This wins the first trick as partner discards the ◇A! How do you continue?

Having found partner with a void in hearts it is clearly correct to carry on with the suit. The question is which heart to lead.

Partner's ◇A discard, with the doubleton in dummy, must indicate a sequence of A-K-Q. Does this give you any ideas? Yes, your ◇J can be an entry! To show this you should lead the ♡9 next, your highest remaining heart to ask for the higher-ranking minor, diamonds. East will probably ruff and may cash one high diamond. If this happens, you will play the ◇7, a high card to encourage a diamond continuation. Now partner should work out that it will be safe to lead a low diamond. This will enable you to get in with the ◇J and lead a third round of hearts. The second heart ruff will put the contract two down.

Note that if South had a singleton diamond, you would need to win the first round of diamonds. A trusting partner would allow you to do this. Note also that if you had a singleton or void in clubs, then you would lead the ♡3 at the second trick. Partner would know from the bidding that your interest in clubs is based on a short suit rather than the ace.

4.2

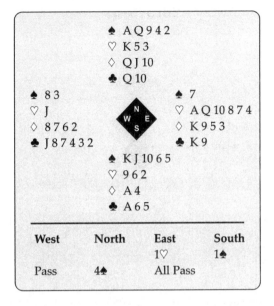

West	North	East	South
		1♡	1♠
Pass	4♠	All Pass	

After this sequence from the rubber bridge table, West leads the ♡J. You overtake with the ♡Q and cash the ♡A, on which West discards a low club. How do you continue?

It was a sensible move overtaking the first round of hearts. This would only be wrong if partner had a doubleton heart and no trumps. That sounds far less likely than a singleton heart and one or two trumps.

As to your play now, you need to play a third round of hearts to kill dummy's king. Your decision, as is usual in this type of situation, is working out what suit you want led back. If you had the ace in one of the minors, it would be clear-cut. Indeed, if you had a minor-suit ace, you might decide to cash it before playing the third round of hearts – you can tell that there is no possibility of an uppercut or a second heart ruff. It would also be clear what to do if you had the ♣J as well as the ♣K. In that case, a lead through dummy's queen would set up a club trick. On the actual layout, asking for a club would not be so bright. One of your best chances of beating the contract lies in finding partner with the ♣J. The last thing you want is for your side to open up the club suit.

Although a diamond return may not do much good, it will surely be safe. Therefore, you lead the ♡10 at the third trick. Partner ruffs and, as requested, leads a diamond. It makes no difference here but, placing South with the ◇A, you will duck. Sooner or later, you will cover the ♣Q with the ♣K and partner's ♣J will take the setting trick.

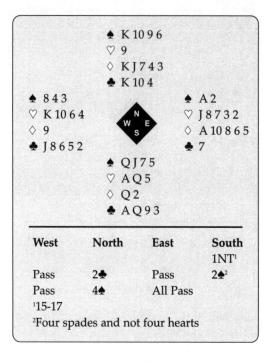

	♠ K 10 9 6		
	♡ 9		
	◇ K J 7 4 3		
	♣ K 10 4		

♠ 8 4 3		♠ A 2
♡ K 10 6 4		♡ J 8 7 3 2
◇ 9		◇ A 10 8 6 5
♣ J 8 6 5 2		♣ 7

	♠ Q J 7 5
	♡ A Q 5
	◇ Q 2
	♣ A Q 9 3

West	North	East	South
			1NT¹
Pass	2♣	Pass	2♠²
Pass	4♠	All Pass	

¹15-17
²Four spades and not four hearts

Partner leads the ◇9 and dummy plays low. What is your plan for four defensive tricks?

So long as South has not opened 1NT with a singleton diamond, you can read the opening lead as a singleton. This makes it tempting to put up the ◇A and fire back a low diamond. You would choose your lowest diamond, the five, because you have no interest in hearts but have some hope of ruffing a club.

Alas, that is not a plan for four tricks, is it? If, having ruffed the second round of diamonds, partner plays ace and another club, you will defeat the contract by two tricks: you score three aces and a ruff each. When, in fact, South has the ♣A, you will score only three: two aces and a ruff.

The knowledge that declarer cannot readily draw trumps, because you hold the ace, opens up a better possibility. After taking the first trick, do not return a diamond. Instead, switch to your singleton club. If partner holds the ♣A, you will crossruff the next two tricks and still beat the contract by two. The gain comes when, as is more likely, South holds that card. You take your ♠A on the first round of trumps and then give your suit-preference signal with the ◇5. Now partner ruffs the diamond and can give you a club ruff to give your side four tricks in all.

4.4

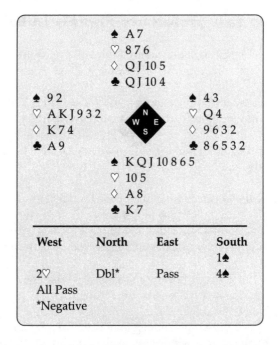

	♠ A 7	
	♡ 8 7 6	
	◇ Q J 10 5	
	♣ Q J 10 4	
♠ 9 2		♠ 4 3
♡ A K J 9 3 2		♡ Q 4
◇ K 7 4		◇ 9 6 3 2
♣ A 9		♣ 8 6 5 3 2
	♠ K Q J 10 8 6 5	
	♡ 10 5	
	◇ A 8	
	♣ K 7	

West	North	East	South
			1♠
2♡	Dbl*	Pass	4♠
All Pass			
*Negative			

You lead the ♡A on which East plays the four and South the five. What are partner's possible heart holdings and how should you continue? Would it make any difference if South had played the ten?

As we discussed in Chapter 1, you expect partner to play high from a doubleton unless it includes the queen (because playing the queen would promise the jack). No matter whether South plays the five or the ten, there are only two possibilities: either the ♡4 is a singleton or it is from Q-4. Partner would not play the four from either 10-4 or 5-4.

If the ♡4 is a singleton, you can beat the contract with two hearts, a heart ruff and the ♣A. More likely, in view of South's spade length, is that the ♡4 comes from Q-4. In this case, you need to score a trick in each minor. A little thought will tell you that you will not get them if you defend passively, say playing king and another heart. Declarer will ruff and, because the ♠A is needed as an entry, knock out the ♣A before drawing trumps. Your opponent will then be able to use dummy's club winners to discard one or more diamonds from hand.

The solution is to lead a low heart at trick two, scarcely caring whether partner ruffs or wins the queen. What is more, you must lead a high heart, the jack or the nine. You want the higher minor back, diamonds, to set up your king. You do not want a club lead to your ace.

Basic Suit-preference Signals in Brief

- A suit-preference signal normally indicates preference between the two suits other than the one now being led and trumps.

- Its most common application is when you lead a suit you know partner cannot return, such as when you give partner a ruff.

- To ask for the higher ranking of the other suits, lead the highest card you can afford.

- To ask for the lower ranking, lead your lowest card.

- You might ask for a suit either if you have a quick entry in the suit, or to set up a winner in that suit, or because you can ruff.

- If you cannot give partner any more ruffs, it might be a good idea to cash a quick winner if it will be the setting trick.

- If no further ruffs are possible, it may better to ask partner to lead a suit that will set up a winner rather than one in which your winner is ready-made.

- You can use a suit-preference signal in a no-trump contract, typically to indicate where you have an entry to your long suit.

Chapter 5
Basic Continuations and Returns

When you lead a suit that you have led before, the appropriate continuation will depend on the nature of your first lead.

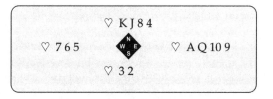

If you have led the middle card from three low (the ♡6), you will normally lead (or play if someone else leads the suit) your highest card (the ♡7) next. This will tell your partner that you do not have a doubleton.

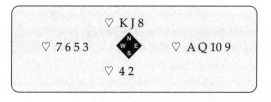

If you have led second highest from four low, you should usually play your original third-highest card next. Although there is some danger that this will look like a doubleton, partner can usually work out from the bidding whether you are more likely to hold four cards or two. The need to differentiate between three cards and four is more important.

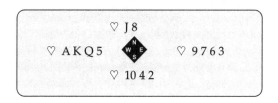

If your first lead was the top of a solid sequence, you generally play the bottom of the sequence on the second round. Partner presumes you have the card just below the one you first lead (the king if you lead the ace), but it is less clear who has the next lower card (here the queen).

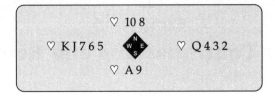

If your holding has become a sequence, again you usually play the lower winning card on the next round. If the six goes to the queen and ace in this side-suit, can you see the advantages of leading the jack? It will be obvious who has the king when the jack holds. This tells East that (a) a third round of the suit might concede a ruff-and-discard, and (b) declarer has no third-round winner in the suit.

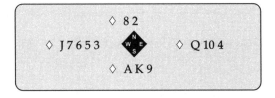

If you have led fourth highest from a five-card suit and are leading low next time, you usually lead your original fifth-highest card. This will tell partner that you started with five. Therefore, if the five goes to the queen and ace, you will lead the three next. As a corollary, if you lead a higher card, partner will assume you started with a three- or four-card suit. Let us see the benefit of this inference in a full deal:

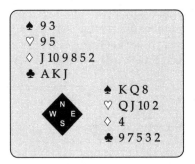

South opens a 15-17 1NT and North raises to 3NT. West leads the ♠4 and your queen drives out the ace. Declarer crosses to the ♣A and runs the ◊J. Partner wins with the king and leads a spade to your king. What will you return if partner's second spade was the two, and what will you return if it is some other spade, say the five?

(i)	(ii)
♠ J 6 5 4 2	♠ J 6 5 4
♡ 8 7 3	♡ A 8 7 3
◊ K 7	◊ K 7
♣ Q 8 4	♣ 10 8 4

The ♣2 on the second round would be consistent for West with (i) here and you should simply continue spades. It is different if West's second spade was higher. In this case, you can make at most three spade tricks and possibly not even that. To beat the contract, partner will need to hold the ♡A, as shown in (ii), and you should switch to the ♡Q.

If you are returning partner's lead, there are two basic rules. Return your highest card if you started with fewer than four cards in the suit. Return your original fourth highest if you started with four or more.

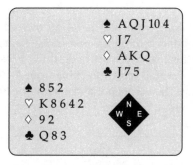

North opens 1♠ and raises South's 1NT response to game. When you lead the ♡4, partner wins with the ace and returns the suit, South playing the ten and then the queen. What do you do?

With A-5-3 East would return the five, highest from an original holding of fewer than four, and with A-9-5-3 the three would be the right card, partner's original fourth highest. Therefore, if the three came back, there is nothing to lose in playing the king. Either the three is from A-3, when the suit is dead, or it comes from A-9-5-3, when declarer has no stopper. If, instead, the five was the card returned, you will know this was not an original fourth best and declarer must have the nine left. In this case you do best to duck the heart so that partner, after gaining the lead with, say, the ♠K, will have a heart to play back. Needless to say, in ducking the heart, you play the ♡2 to show a five-card suit.

The knowledge that partner would return high from three might also help you to tell the difference between a tripleton and a doubleton.

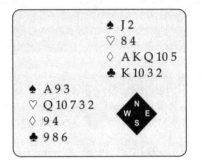

♠ J 2
♡ 8 4
◇ A K Q 10 5
♣ K 10 3 2

♠ A 9 3
♡ Q 10 7 3 2
◇ 9 4
♣ 9 8 6

North opens 1◇, South responds 1♠ and North rebids 2♣. Then South bids 2NT and North raises to game. You lead the ♡3, which goes to the four, ace and five. Back comes the ♡6 covered by the jack and queen. How should you continue?

Firstly, you place South with the ♡K (a) on the bidding and (b) from East's failure to play this card on the first trick – remember you play the king from A-K in third seat. Who do you think possesses the ♡9? The knowledge that East would return the nine from A-9-6 tells you: it is in declarer's hand. Thus there is no point in continuing hearts. Your best bet is to exit passively with a diamond.

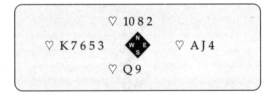

♡ 10 8 2

♡ K 7 6 5 3   ♡ A J 4

♡ Q 9

Of course, if you see that returning your highest card from an original three-card holding may cost a trick, you do not do it. As East, if you win the first round with the ace, it would be a mistake to play back the jack. Doing so will set up dummy's ten on the third round if partner has led from the king.

The opposite type of exception you can see at the top of the next page. As East, it would be foolhardy to win the first round with the ace and play back the four. Declarer could let this run round to dummy and score an undeserved trick in the suit. Your correct return is the jack.

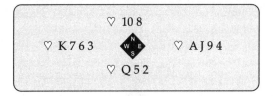

On our final layout below, you are West. You cash the ace-king of this side suit, seeing East play high-low and South drop the queen. If you do not want partner to ruff next time, you had better continue with the jack. Any other card may cause East to place South with Q-J-x.

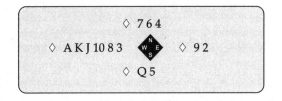

Test Yourself

5.1

		♠ 9 7 5 4	
		♡ 4 3	
		◇ Q 10 7 4	
		♣ A 9 4	
♠ K Q J 10			♠ 3
♡ J 10 8 7 6 5			♡ A K Q 2
◇ K 5 3			◇ J 8 6 2
♣ —			♣ K 8 6 2
		♠ A 8 6 2	
		♡ 9	
		◇ A 9	
		♣ Q J 10 7 5 3	

West	North	East	South
			1♣
1♡	Dbl *	4♡	4♠
Dbl	All Pass		
*Negative			

When West leads the ♠K, how might the defenders take nine or ten tricks?

5.2

	♠ J 8 3		
	♡ A K J 5		
	◊ K		
	♣ J 10 8 5 3		

♠ Q 7 4
♡ 10 8 3
◊ Q 10 8 3 2
♣ 4 2

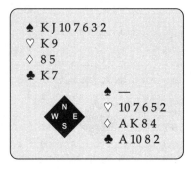

West	North	East	South
			1NT*
Pass	2♣	Pass	2◊
Pass	3NT	All Pass	
*12-14			

You lead the ◊3 and are pleased when partner wins with the ace and returns the four. South plays the nine on the second round and you win with the ten. How do you continue? Would it make any difference if partner had returned the ◊7?

5.3

♠ K J 10 7 6 3 2
♡ K 9
◊ 8 5
♣ K 7

♠ —
♡ 10 7 6 5 2
◊ A K 8 4
♣ A 10 8 2

South opens 1♠ and North bids 2NT, showing a game-forcing spade raise. After South makes a waiting bid of 3♠, denying a singleton, North makes a cue-bid of 4♣ and South one of 4♡. Both cue bids show first- or second-round control of the suit bid (ace, king, singleton or void). North then signs off in 4♠.

Partner leads the ◊Q against 4♠ and you decide to overtake with the king. What do you return?

Solutions

5.1

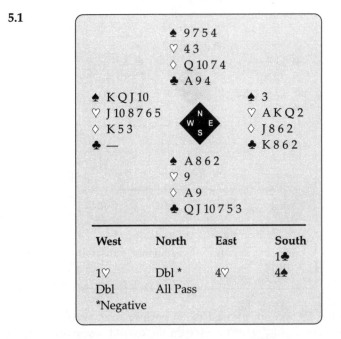

	♠ 9 7 5 4		
	♡ 4 3		
	◇ Q 10 7 4		
	♣ A 9 4		

♠ K Q J 10		♠ 3
♡ J 10 8 7 6 5		♡ A K Q 2
◇ K 5 3		◇ J 8 6 2
♣ —		♣ K 8 6 2

	♠ A 8 6 2		
	♡ 9		
	◇ A 9		
	♣ Q J 10 7 5 3		

West	North	East	South
			1♣
1♡	Dbl *	4♡	4♠
Dbl	All Pass		
*Negative			

West leads the ♠K, which presumably holds the first trick. Can you see how the defenders might take nine or even ten tricks?

The key comes at the second trick. West continues with specifically the ♠10. Since the lead announced possession of the K-Q and most likely the jack as well, East can read West for K-Q-J-10. This raises the possibility of drawing all of declarer's (and dummy's) trumps. On the second round East throws the ♡A, top of a sequence, and let us say that South wins. If the club finesse works, it will be possible to salvage a bit from the wreckage and accordingly declarer leads the ♣Q.

There would be no point in ruffing a loser and West has two choices here: to discourage diamonds with the ◇3 or give a more positive signal for hearts with the ♡J – remember East's ♡A discard probably shows the A-K-Q, making West's holding solid. In any event, dummy's ace wins and East takes the second round of clubs with the king. To extract a big penalty now East needs to lead a low heart – not so tough if West has thrown the ♡J or could be trusted to have thrown a heart if not holding the ♡J. West gains the lead and draws two more rounds of trumps, on which East unblocks the ♡K and ♡Q. West then finishes the hearts.

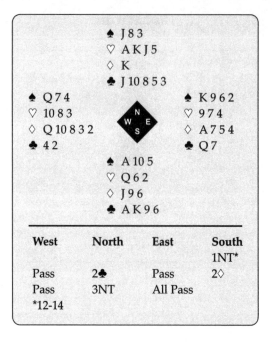

West	North	East	South
			1NT*
Pass	2♣	Pass	2◊
Pass	3NT	All Pass	
*12-14			

You lead the ◊3 and are pleased when partner wins with the ace and returns the four. South plays the nine on the second round and you win with the ten. How do you continue? Would it make any difference if partner had returned the ◊7?

How do you read the diamond position when partner returns the four? Since you have the two, this can only be from a four-card suit or A-4. Given that East might have switched if South has five diamonds, and that then you may be unable to beat the contract in any event, you play for the first possibility. This is not the moment to tell partner that you have five diamonds by leading the two. This will be costly if South's last diamond is the jack. Instead, cash the queen, trusting that, with an original holding of A-J-7-4 or A-J-5-4, partner would unblock the jack.

If partner returns the ◊7, you will know South has four diamonds (at least). The only way the seven could be East's four-highest diamond is with a holding of A-J-9-7, which becomes impossible when South covers. In this case, you will not want to play a third round of diamonds but will hope partner can do so. Given the strong hearts in dummy, you would switch to a spade. Finding partner with the ♠A is probably the only way to defeat the contract. If you defend passively, then declarer, if holding the ♡Q, may well have nine tricks ready to run: five clubs and four hearts.

```
                    ♠ K J 10 7 6 3 2
                    ♡ K 9
                    ◇ 10 5
                    ♣ K 7
    ♠ 9                              ♠ —
    ♡ Q 8 4          ┌───┐          ♡ 10 7 6 5 2
    ◇ Q J 9 7 2      │ N │          ◇ A K 8 4
    ♣ Q 9 6 3      W │   │ E        ♣ A 10 8 2
                     │ S │
                    ♠ A Q 8 5 4
                    ♡ A J 3
                    ◇ 6 3
                    ♣ J 5 4
```

West	North	East	South
			1♠
Pass	2NT[1]	Pass	3♠
Pass	4♣[2]	Pass	4♡[2]
Pass	4♠	All Pass	

[1]Game-forcing spade raise
[2]Cue bids (first or second-round control)

West leads the ◇Q and you decide to overtake with the king. What do you return?

Suppose firstly that you cash the ◇A at trick two. What will you lead after that? A club will set up dummy's king and a heart would be highly dangerous if partner has the queen but not the jack. South, with ♡A-J-x, will play low and West will have to play the queen.

It is better to return a low diamond and, since you started with four cards in the suit, you play the four, your original fourth best. This must be safe because South, who has denied a singleton, cannot hold five diamonds. In any event, a lead from Q-x would be unusual.

Partner, upon winning the diamond, will be aware that South could be out of the suit and that leading a third round would concede a ruff-and-discard. Given that you might have doubled 4♣ with the ♣A and ♣J, and that South's 4♡ cue-bid means you cannot hold the ♡A and ♡J, partner should work out what to do. This is to do something you cannot do, namely to exit with a trump. Now, whether declarer finesses in hearts or tries a club to the king, the contract fails.

Basic Continuations and Returns in Brief

- If you have led fourth highest and are leading low next time, play your original fifth-highest card.

- If you have led middle from three low, play the top card on the next round unless you want people to think you started with a doubleton.

- If you have led second highest from four low, it is normal to play your original third-highest card on the second round to distinguish your holding from a three-card suit.

- If you have led from, or now have, a sequence, you usually lead the lowest of your remaining high touching cards.

- If, however, partner may be out of the suit in which you hold a sequence and you wish to avoid a ruff, lead a card partner will know is a winner.

- In returning partner's suit from an original holding of three cards (or fewer), you usually return your highest card.

- In returning partner's suit from an original four-card or longer holding, you usually return your original fourth-highest card.

- Pay careful attention to both partner's cards and declarer's on the early rounds of a suit. This will frequently allow you to judge whether partner's return is high or low.

- Nobody expects you to give tricks away to signal your length on either a return or a continuation. If you need to lead either high or low to avoid losing a trick, go ahead and do it.

- If you allow partner to win a trick that you could win yourself, it is often a signal that you want partner to make a play that you could not make.

Chapter 6
Basics of Leading New Suits

On switching to a new suit, you often lead the same card as on the opening lead. You lead top of a sequence, fourth highest from a long suit with strength in it and a higher card from a weak suit.

If you are West and switch to this suit, you lead the jack. If you are East and do so, the normal lead is the three.

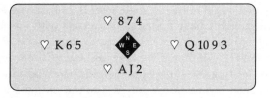

This time the normal switch from West is the five while from East it is the ten. These leads stop the jack from scoring.

If you are West and switch to this suit, then you follow the normal lead convention of high from a doubleton. If you are East, the usual card is the seven, although you might deviate from that if you think West has the king and you want to induce declarer to finesse.

Sometimes the appearance of a particular holding in dummy will tell you not to make the normal lead:

With an interior sequence (e.g. K-J-10, Q-10-9), the normal card to lead is the top of the touching cards rather than the top card. Here, as East, though, you switch to the queen, rather than the ten, to kill North's jack. This may well save a trick if South has K-x-x, A-K-x or similar.

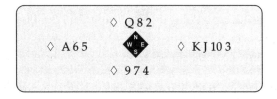

If you lead from K-J-10-x on the first trick, you start with the jack. Can you see why that might not be so good here? If, as East, you lead the suit at all, you presumably have reason to place West with the ace. Leading the jack might cost a trick if South holds 9-x-x-x. Here it also causes a problem for West. If South had the king and you J-10-9-x with an entry elsewhere for leading the suit again, it would work best to let the jack run. On the actual layout, you want West to put up the ace and play a diamond back. This makes leading low right on both counts.

As East, if you lead a diamond, it is likely to be right to underlead your ace against either a suit or a no-trump contract. In a suit contract, you hope for two tricks either if West has the king, or if declarer has the king and jack but guesses to try the jack. Defending a no-trump contract, you might set your sights higher. Facing K-J-9-x or K-J-10-x your side can take four tricks. Partner wins the first round cheaply, puts you back in with the ace, and you can lead a third round. How does partner know it is safe to return the suit? Your lead of a low card indicates strength in the suit and, if it is reasonable for partner to do so, asks for the suit back.

Let us see an extension of this principle in the context of a full deal.

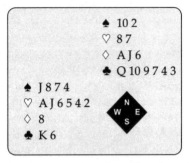

South opens 2NT and North raises to 3NT. You lead the ♡5, East plays the ten and the king wins. Declarer crosses to the ◊A and runs the ♣Q to your king. How do you read the heart layout and how do you continue?

Playing 'third-hand high' partner would not play the ten from Q-10-(x), so South must have the ♡Q. Nor is a holding of 10-9-x possible. With that, partner would play the nine, not the ten. This tells you that South holds the ♡Q and ♡9, and that you cannot run the suit. The best bet is to lead a spade hoping that partner has the ace and can return the ♡3 to let you run the suit. Can you see why it matters which spade you lead?

Suppose your actual hand were something like this:

♠ K J 7 4
♡ J 9 6 5 4 2
◊ 8
♣ K 6

With that alternative hand, you would want partner to win the spade and return the suit rather than revert to hearts. It follows that the size of the spade you lead must indicate whether you want a spade back or not. Partner is not interested in merely knowing whether you hold the ♠J. On your actual hand, you do not want a spade back and switch to the ♠8. With the alternative hand, you would switch to the ♠4. In both cases partner should get the right message.

There are other ways to tell partner what to lead. If you have an ace-king combination, you might cash the king before leading some other suit.

Why do you lead the king from ace-king when to the first trick you lead the ace from ace-king? The answer is twofold. On the opening lead, it is rare that you can tell it is safe to lead an unsupported ace and your partner can therefore assume that the ace shows the king. By contrast, later in the play you might need to lead an unsupported ace and you do not want partner to think you have the king has well. Besides, if you are the opening leader, it is unlikely that you hold an ace-king combination that you failed to lead initially.

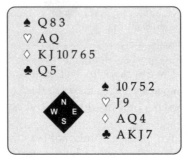

You open a strong 1NT as East, South overcalls with 2♡ and North raises to 3♡. West leads the ◊2 and you take the jack with the queen. Reading the lead as a singleton (you can see all the diamonds down to the ten), you cash the ◊A and partner discards a low club. What do you lead next?

You may recall from Chapter 4 that when giving partner a ruff you give a suit-preference signal, leading high to ask for the higher unplayed side-suit and low to ask for the lower unplayed side-suit. Here this will not work. You only have one diamond left, which means partner cannot place any suit-preference connotations on it. Fortunately, you have an easy way to sidestep this problem. Before leading a third round of diamonds, cash the ♣K Even without the agreement that you lead king from ace-king after the first trick it will be obvious, when the king wins, with the ♣Q in dummy, that you hold the ♣A as well. Now if you give partner a ruff it will be clear to lead a club next. In fact, you could probably cash the ♣A after the king. If you trust partner to give you a length signal, playing high from an original six-card holding, you will know whether the ♣A will stand up.

Needless to say, if your hand were a bit different, say with ♠A-K-7-2 and ♣J-10-7-6, you would cash a top spade at trick three. The key point is not to play a third round of diamonds prematurely. If you did that and partner returned the wrong black suit, declarer could draw trumps ending in dummy and run the rest of the diamonds.

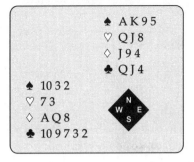

```
              ♠ A K 9 5
              ♡ Q J 8
              ◊ J 9 4
              ♣ Q J 4
  ♠ 10 3 2                    N
  ♡ 7 3                   W       E
  ◊ A Q 8                     S
  ♣ 10 9 7 3 2
```

South opens 1♡, North responds 1♠ and South rebids 2◊. North's arguably precipitate jump to 4♡ then ends the bidding.

You lead the ♣10, which goes jack, king, six. Partner switches to the ◊6 and you win with queen. You cash the ◊A and all follow. How do you continue if East's second diamond is the three and what do you do if it is the seven instead?

Since declarer did not capture the ♣K with the ace, you can place partner with this card. This makes it tempting to play the ♣9 next (not that it matters which club you lead on this deal). Whether this is a good idea depends on what happened on the second round of diamonds. Here are a couple of possible hands for partner:

(i)	(ii)
♠ J 8 6 4	♠ J 8 6 4
♡ 9 6 2	♡ 9 6 2
◊ 6 3	◊ 7 6 3
♣ A K 8 5	♣ A K 5

Holding the first hand ,partner would play the three on the second round of diamonds to complete a high-low signal. In this case, you should carry on with a third round of the suit. With only one club trick available to your side, it takes a ruff to defeat the contract.

With the second hand, partner must do the opposite, playing upwards on the second round with the ◊7 to make sure you do not think there is a ruff on. If this happens, you revert to clubs and again you take the first four tricks. You can see from this that it was important partner did not switch to the ◊7, the old-fashioned 'top-of-nothing' lead. The ◊7 followed by either the ◊6 or the ◊3 would look like a doubleton.

Test Yourself

6.1 (a)

♡ 8 6 2

♡ Q J 9 4

As East, you decide to switch to a heart – often a good idea up to a weak suit in dummy. Which card should you lead?

6.1 (b)

♠ 10 9 3

♠ Q J 6 5 4

You are East and have decided it is right to switch to this suit. Suppose the contract is 4♡ and your side needs quick spade tricks. Which card will you lead? Might it make any difference if the contract is 1NT and your side needs five spade tricks?

6.2

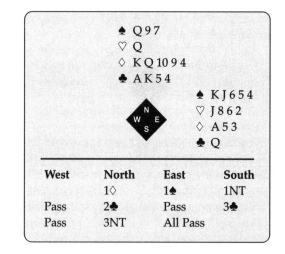

♠ Q 9 7
♡ Q
◇ K Q 10 9 4
♣ A K 5 4

♠ K J 6 5 4
♡ J 8 6 2
◇ A 5 3
♣ Q

West	North	East	South
	1◇	1♠	1NT
Pass	2♣	Pass	3♣
Pass	3NT	All Pass	

Partner leads the ♠10 and you win the trick by taking dummy's queen with your king. Which card do you return? Would you lead something else if your spades were K-J-8-6-4 and your hearts were 9-8-6-2?

6.3

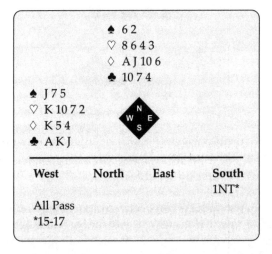

	♠ 62		
	♡ 8643		
	◇ AJ 10 6		
	♣ 10 7 4		

♠ J 7 5
♡ K 10 7 2
◇ K 5 4
♣ A K J

West	North	East	South
			1NT*
All Pass			
*15-17			

You decide to lead the ♡2 and partner's ♡A wins. Back comes the ♡J, covered by the queen and king. How do you place the missing high cards and how should you continue?

6.4

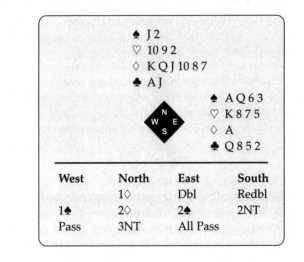

	♠ J 2		
	♡ 10 9 2		
	◇ K Q J 10 8 7		
	♣ A J		

♠ A Q 6 3
♡ K 8 7 5
◇ A
♣ Q 8 5 2

West	North	East	South
	1◇	Dbl	Redbl
1♠	2◇	2♠	2NT
Pass	3NT	All Pass	

Partner leads the ♣4 and your ace wins. Which card do you return? Would it make any difference if you had ♠A-9-6-3 and ♡K-J-7-5?

Solutions

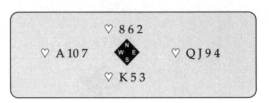

♡ 8 6 2

♡ A 10 7   ♡ Q J 9 4

♡ K 5 3

As East, you decide to switch to a heart – often a good idea up to a weak suit in dummy. Which card should you lead?

Let us see what happens if you lead your fourth-highest heart, the four. Unless there is a particular hurry to gain the lead, declarer will duck and the ten wins. Partner, however, cannot safely continue the suit. It is much better to lead top of your slightly imperfect sequence. If your queen holds, you will retain the lead and can play a second round. If there are no trumps and either you have a side entry or declarer covers on the second round, you will end up with four heart tricks.

6.1 (b)

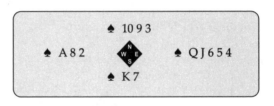

♠ 10 9 3

♠ A 8 2   ♠ Q J 6 5 4

♠ K 7

As East you have decided to switch to this suit. Suppose the contract is 4♡ and your side needs quick tricks. Which card will you lead?

The queen is the right lead. You can only ever make two spade tricks if South has a doubleton. If you find partner with A-x, by leading the ♠Q there is a chance of a ruff on the third round.

If the contract is 1NT and your side needs five spade tricks, there is little point in switching to the queen. Unless partner has the ace and king, declarer is bound to have a stopper. Just as you lead low on the first trick from Q-J-x-x-x against a no-trump contract, you lead the five now. Since it would be essential to play the king if you had the ♠A, it is highly likely that declarer will go up with the ♠K from K-x. On the actual layout, this allows you to run the entire spade suit.

	♠ Q 9 7	
	♡ Q	
	◇ K Q 10 9 4	
	♣ A K 5 4	

♠ 10 2		♠ K J 6 5 4
♡ K 10 7 4 3	N	♡ J 8 6 2
◇ 8 6	W E	◇ A 5 3
♣ J 10 7 3	S	♣ Q

	♠ A 8 3	
	♡ A 9 5	
	◇ J 7 2	
	♣ 9 8 6 2	

West	North	East	South
	1◇	1♠	1NT
Pass	2♣	Pass	3♣
Pass	3NT	All Pass	

Partner leads the ♣10 and you win the trick by taking dummy's queen with your king. Which card do you return?

Your poor spade intermediates make it clear that you stand little hope of setting up the suit. Declarer must have a double stopper and, since West would lead low from 10-x-x, communications are going to present a problem. Even if partner has an entry and comes in before your ◇A is gone, the spade suit is dead. It must be a better bet to switch to a heart. If you can find partner with the king and ten or the ace and ten, declarer should have only one heart stopper.

On the opening lead, you would lead the two from J-8-6-2 and you have no reason to do anything different. Remember that the lead of a low card during the play indicates that you have some strength in the suit and, in general, that you do not mind if partner continues the suit. When this happens, you will defeat the contract by two tricks as the cards lie.

Would you lead something else if your spades were K-J-8-6-4 and your hearts 9-8-6-2? In this case, your plan is quite different. All you need is for partner to get in and lead a second spade and you can be almost certain that the contract will fail. The whole spade suit will run after you get in with the ◇A. To indicate a disinterest in hearts you would lead the ♡8, again the same card you would choose if you had the opening lead and had decided to lead a heart.

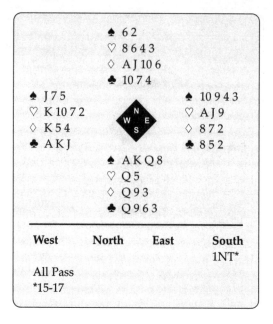

| ♠ 62 |
| ♡ 8643 |
| ◊ A J 10 6 |
| ♣ 10 7 4 |

West	North	East	South
			1NT*
All Pass			
*15-17			

You decide to lead the ♡2 and partner's ♡A wins. Back comes the ♡J, covered by the queen and king. How do you place the missing high cards and how should you continue?

You do not need any signals to work out who has the missing high cards. South's bid announced a minimum of 15 points, there are 5 in dummy and you started with 15. This puts East with a maximum of 5, all of which you have seen.

With the ◊Q on your right, declarer very probably has four diamond tricks to go with the ♠A-K-Q. Even if partner has four diamonds, you cannot beat the contract if South has the ♡9 because then the ♡9 and ♡8 will be equals against your ♡10. It therefore makes sense to place partner with the ♡9. (This is likely in any event because, with only two hearts and knowing that your lead of the ♡2 must be from a four-card suit, East would probably have switched.) In this case, your side can take the first seven tricks with four hearts and three clubs.

Of course, if you lead the ♡7 to partner's hoped-for ♡9, you cannot be sure of getting a club return. After all, you could hold much better spades and much worse clubs than you do. Also, thinking you might have tenaces in both black suits, partner may not give the matter much thought. The solution is to cash the ♣K first. This way it will be clear that you want a club back.

```
                    ♠ J 2
                    ♡ 10 9 2
                    ◇ K Q J 10 8 7
                    ♣ A J
  ♠ 10 8 5 4              N        ♠ A Q 6 3
  ♡ Q 6 4          W          E    ♡ K 8 7 5
  ◇ 5 4 3 2              S        ◇ A
  ♣ 9 4                            ♣ Q 8 5 2
                    ♠ K 9 7
                    ♡ A J 3
                    ◇ 9 6
                    ♣ K 10 7 6 3
```

West	North	East	South
	1◇	Dbl	Redbl
1♠	2◇	2♠	2NT
Pass	3NT	All Pass	

Partner leads the ♠4 and your ace wins. Which card do you return?

There are two clues as to what to do here. The first is partner's lead of the ♠4. Since you can see the ♠2 in dummy and the ♠3 in your hand, you know the lead comes from a four-card suit. The second is South's bid of 2NT, which surely promises a spade stopper, the king no doubt. This tells you that, if you return the ♠Q, your side will make at most three spade tricks. (Obviously, you do not consider leading the ♠3 with the jack now bare in dummy). Unfortunately, three spade tricks and the ◇A will not be enough to defeat the contract. What you need to do is to steal a heart trick, possible if partner has ♡Q-x-x, before clearing the spades. With a heart trick as well, three spades and a diamond will give you five in all.

The snag, as hinted in the question, is that partner may think you are giving up on spades altogether and trying to set up the hearts. To make it clear that you do not want a heart back, switch to the ♡8. South, with ♡A-J-x, has to duck.

Would it make any difference if you had ♠A-9-6-3 and ♡K-J-7-5? In this case it would still be correct to switch to a heart because you are unlikely to beat the contract if South has the ace-queen over your king. Now, however, you have no reason to discourage a heart return, and should lead your normal fourth-highest card, the ♡5.

Basics of Leading New Suits in Brief

- In general, the same conventions apply on a switch to a new suit as to the initial lead.

- Lead top of a sequence or the highest touching card from an interior sequence.

- With some strength but not a strong sequence, lead low – your fourth-highest card if you have four or more cards in the suit.

- With only low cards, lead top of a doubleton or second highest from a longer holding.

- If you do not want a suit returned, lead a high spot card, just as if you had only low cards in the suit.

- If the cards you see in dummy make it likely that leading your normal card will cost a trick, lead a card that will not cost.

- After the first trick, the lead of the ace does not signify the king and partner normally encourages only if holding the king.

Chapter 7
More on Following to Partner's Lead

If partner returns your suit, the position is like that when you follow to partner's lead or continue the suit yourself. When trying to win the trick, or to force out a high card from dummy, play the lower of touching cards. If you have led from a five-card suit and are not trying to win the trick, you play your lowest card on the second round.

You lead the ♡3 and the jack fetches the ace. If East returns the six and South plays the nine, you play the ten. Remember, with the jack gone, your queen and ten are equals. If you played the queen, partner might put South with A-10-9, in which case your side has no heart tricks.

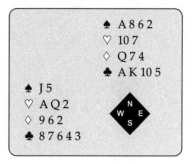

South plays in 4♠ on the sequence 1♣ – 1♠ – 2♠ – 4♠. You lead the ◊6, partner wins with the king and returns the ace. What do you do?

Play upwards with the nine. You do not want partner to try to give you a ruff, which might be needed if you had ♡A-9-2 and a doubleton ◊6-2.

The time has come to move across to the East seat.

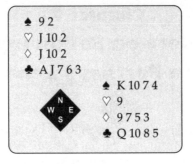

South plays in 4♡ after another uninterrupted sequence, 1♡ – 2♡ – 4♡. When West leads the ♣Q, do you think you should encourage?

Although the king and ten are nice cards, it would not be good to play the seven (or the ten). Partner has not overcalled in spades, making it likely that declarer has at least three spades and intends to ruff one in dummy. Rather than risk that declarer allows the ♣Q to win, overtake with the king. If your luck is in, West will have something like ♡A-Q-x and be able to draw dummy's trumps when, if your ♠K wins, you lead a trump. If declarer takes the ♠K with the ace and returns the suit, West needs to think. Since you could ill afford to overtake the first spade unless you also had the ♠10, West should duck to let you win.

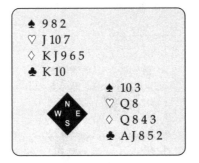

South opens 1♡ and North's raise to 2♡ buys the contract. What do you do when partner leads the ♠A?

From partner's failure to overcall 1♠ or reopen with 2♠, it is clear that West and South have four spades each. If you encourage, your side may take two spades, a ruff and the ♣A – no good. It must be better to play the ♠3. You hope partner has the ♣Q and ♠A-K-J-x. Then, after a club switch (low to show the queen), you can score two clubs, three spades and, by overruffing the fourth round of spades, the ♡Q.

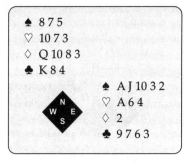

South opens 2NT and North's raise to 3NT closes the auction. It seems to be your lucky day because partner places the ♠9 on the table.

The lead is clearly top of a doubleton, marking South with K-Q-x and two spade stoppers. Since you have only one entry, you need to duck the first trick in the hope that partner gets in before you have to part with the ♡A. The question is how to encourage a spade continuation. Although you could try playing the ♠3, even the most attentive of partners may fail to read it as a high card. The better play is to overtake with the ♠10. This must show a strong spade holding because, with 8-7-x in dummy, it could cost a trick to play the ten from J-10-x-x.

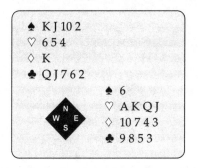

South opens a 15-17 1NT in second seat, rebids 2♠ over North's 2♣ inquiry, and plays in 4♠. What do you do when West leads the ♡10?

The normal rule is to play the lower or, in this case, lowest of equals. This indicates playing the jack. The danger, however, of playing the jack, cashing the ace and leading the queen is that (because of your initial pass) declarer will place West with all the missing high cards. It will then be simple to get a two-way trump finesse right or even drop a singleton ♣K offside. It is much better to win with the ace and continue with the queen and jack, making it look like West has the ♡K.

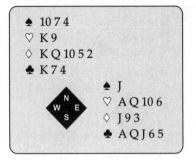

This time South opens 1♠, North responds 2◇ and you double for take-out. South rebids 2♠ and North's raise to 3♠ ends the bidding. Partner leads the ♣2 and dummy plays low.

One option is to play for the ♣2 to be a singleton, in which case you can give West a ruff. Given South's spade length, though, it is more likely the lead comes from 10-x-x. In this case, you will need partner to have a trump trick. Moreover, you will need partner to switch to hearts after making that trump trick because South can hold at most two clubs. To deter a club continuation, win with the ♣Q not the ♣J.

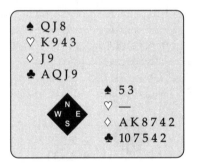

This time West opens 3♡, South reopens with 3♠ after two passes, and North raises to 4♠. West leads the ◇6.

On the previous deals you played high from touching cards to deceive declarer and then to tell a white lie to partner. Can you see another reason to do so? An unusual play normally means an unusual holding, here your heart void. If the lead is a singleton, you will want partner to ruff the next diamond, cash the ♡A and give you a heart ruff. You could win the first diamond and return the eight, but that would backfire if West has a doubleton diamond and a trump trick. Best is to play the ◇A and return the king, hoping partner gets the message.

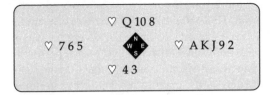

On the first deal of the chapter, we saw that, if partner returns a suit from which you have led the middle of three cards, you normally play upwards. You might make an exception if you want to fool everyone into thinking you have a doubleton, either if you cannot stand a switch from partner or, as may be the case here, you want declarer to ruff the third round high. So, having led the ♡6 to the ♡J, you might play the ♡5 underneath partner's high heart return.

If you have led second highest from four small, you usually drop the third highest on the second round. Assuming it is clear you cannot hold a doubleton, this will tell partner that you have more than three cards in the suit. Dropping either the highest card or your lowest would be a suit-preference signal. Here, if the first trick goes six, eight, nine, ace, you will normally play the five if East gets in and returns the queen.

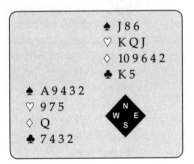

South opens 1◊, North raises to 3◊ and South rebids 3NT. You lead the ♠3 and are pleased to see partner take the king and return the five. South, who played the seven the first time, now plays the queen. How do you read the spade position, and how should you play?

Partner would not return the five from ♠K-10-5 and must have begun with a doubleton. This means the only way you can run the suit is if you can gain the lead. If you do not think that is very likely, you want to take the second spade and switch to a club in the hope partner has good clubs, say A-J-10-x, and an entry. Unfortunately, that does not leave South much in the way of high cards, making it a better bet to hope that your ◇Q provides an entry. So that declarer is not tempted to take an avoidance play in diamonds (low to the king with K-J-x-x or low to the ace with A-J-x-x), conceal the ♣2, playing the ♣4 instead. Thinking the spades are 4-3, declarer may now take a finesse into your hand.

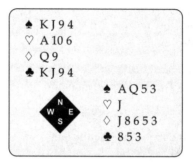

After North-South bid 1♡ – 1♠ — 2♡ – 4♡, West leads the ◇A. You play the three, showing (in view of dummy's holding) an odd number rather than discouragement. Partner continues with the ◇K.

The odds are high that partner intends to switch at the next trick, either to avoid conceding a ruff-and-discard or simply to keep the initiative. Can you make sure this is to a spade rather than a club? You may have guessed the answer: by using a suit-preference signal. Excluding diamonds, the suit being played now, and the trump suit, leaves the two black suits. The higher of these is spades and you should therefore follow with a high diamond: the highest you can afford, the eight.

```
♠ 6 5 3
♡ 9
◇ J 8 6 5 3
♣ A Q 5 3
```

If this were your hand, you would want a club switch. In this case, you would play your lowest diamond left, the five. What would you do with values in both black suits? You would play a middling card, the ◇6.

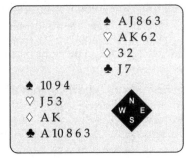

Here partner opens 3◊, North reopens with a double after two passes, and South's 4♡ closes the auction. After the ◊K collects the two, queen and four, you lead the ◊A, on which go the three, seven and nine.

East knows you will not (indeed cannot) continue diamonds and should therefore have given a suit preference signal on the second round of the suit. In the context of what you can see, a high card (the ◊J) would suggest the ♠K while a low one (the ◊5) would suggest the ♣K. The actual card played, the ◊7 was neither of these, which means South has both the ♠K and the ♣K. Your best bet is to exit passively with a trump in the hope that partner has both black queens.

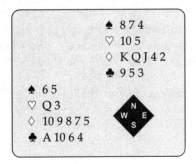

This time East opens 4♡ and 4♠ from South buys the contract. You lead the ♡Q, which wins when partner plays the jack and declarer the nine.

Even without the ♡10 on view in dummy, the ♡J would be an unusual card to play. Why not overtake in case your ♡Q is a singleton? You may be getting the message by now that an unusual card conveys a special meaning: suit-preference. Since the ♡J is high, it asks for the higher minor, diamonds. Partner presumably has a void in the suit. This makes it your turn to give a suit-preference signal. Wanting a club back, you switch to your lowest diamond, the five.

In this situation, in which partner has a fistful of hearts from which to play, you might also take the ♡2 on the first trick as a suit-preference signal. Simply to signal an odd number of hearts it would be necessary for partner to play a low card but not the very lowest.

Let us go back to the East seat and see if you can work out what type of signal you should give on the opening lead:

```
              ♠ A 10 2
              ♡ 10 8 4
              ◇ A 9
              ♣ Q J 10 6 5
                              ♠ K 7 4
                     N        ♡ 9 2
                  W     E     ◇ Q 10 7 4 3
                     S        ♣ 9 7 2
```

The opponents bid 1♡ – 2♣ – 3♣ – 3♡ – 4♡. Partner leads the ♣A.

In view of the fact that North-South have bid and raised clubs, the lead comes as something of a surprise. To justify the lead partner surely has a singleton club. This means that a switch is coming and you need to give suit-preference, not attitude or count. You have no quick entry, but your ♠K figures to be a winner on the second round whether or not partner has any help in the suit. This means you should ask for a spade switch by playing the ♣9. With any luck, West will switch to a spade and, even if the ace goes up, there is a chance that declarer has a fast trump to lose. Then partner will win, play a spade to your king and ruff the second round of clubs.

```
              ♠ Q 7 4
              ♡ 9 2
              ◇ K 10 7 4 3
              ♣ 9 7 2
```

If this were your hand, you would feel more optimistic about your prospects after a diamond switch and so would play your lowest club, the two. You may have guessed what you would do with equal holdings in the pointed suits, say the ♠Q and the ◇Q. You would play your middle club, the seven, and hope partner works out the position.

Perhaps the most common time for giving a suit-preference signal on the opening lead is the one I have saved until last. Again, we consider the position from the viewpoint of the defender giving the signal.

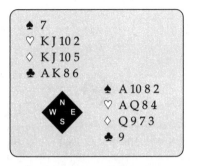

The bidding is short and simple: 3♣ from South and 5♣ from North. When West leads the ♠K, you can see the cards above.

Dummy's spade holding makes it clear to all concerned that there is little future in continuing the suit. A switch will be in order. With the similar holdings in dummy in the red suits, partner will, without a signal, be on a guess as to which one to lead. Since you want the higher suit, you play the highest spade you can afford, in this case the ten. It is just too bad if declarer has a singleton heart.

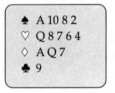

Needless to say, if this were your hand, you would play your lowest spade, the two, to ask for the lower red suit, diamonds.

Finally, if you could not tell which suit you want, you would play the neutral eight. This would say that you have either strength in both red suits or weakness in both, and West may be able to work out what to do from that. Actually, on occasion you might want a spade continuation to play safe or force the dummy. In this case, you might try the middling eight and hope partner works out the position. A safer bet, however, might be to overtake with the ♠A and continue spades yourself. Bear in mind the implication of leaving partner on lead when you do not have to: it is that you want something done you cannot do yourself.

Test Yourself

7.1

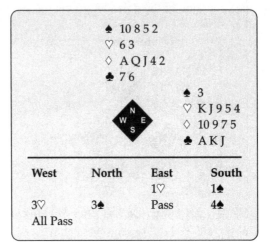

	♠ 10 8 5 2		
	♡ 6 3		
	◊ A Q J 4 2		
	♣ 7 6		

		♠ 3
		♡ K J 9 5 4
		◊ 10 9 7 5
		♣ A K J

West	North	East	South
		1♡	1♠
3♡	3♠	Pass	4♠
All Pass			

Partner leads the ◊3 and declarer plays low from dummy. What do you play and why?

7.2

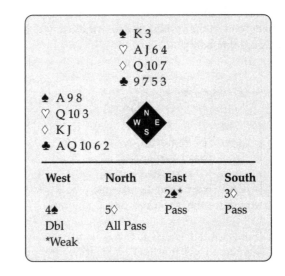

	♠ K 3
	♡ A J 6 4
	◊ Q 10 7
	♣ 9 7 5 3

| ♠ A 9 8 |
| ♡ Q 10 3 |
| ◊ K J |
| ♣ A Q 10 6 2 |

West	North	East	South
		2♣*	3◊
4♠	5◊	Pass	Pass
Dbl	All Pass		
*Weak			

You lead the ♠A, on which go the three, two and five. What meaning do you attribute to partner's ♠2 and what do you lead next?

7.3

	♠ K 8 3	
	♡ J 10 6	
	◊ K 6 3 2	
	♣ Q 10 3	

		♠ J 7
		♡ K Q 4 2
W N E		◊ A Q
S		♣ 9 7 6 4 2

West	North	East	South
		1♣[1]	1♠
Dbl[2]	2♠	Pass	4♠
All Pass			
[1]May be short			
[2]Negative			

Partner leads the ♡8 and dummy covers with the ten. What card do you play and why?

7.4

	♠ K 6 4	
	♡ A Q 10	
	◊ A K Q J 5	
	♣ 9 8	

♠ A 10		
♡ 8 7 2		
◊ 9 3	W N E	
♣ A K J 7 6 2	S	

West	North	East	South
1♣	Dbl	Pass	1♠
2♣	2◊	Pass	2♠
Pass	3♠	Pass	4♠
All Pass			

Your lead of the ♣A collects the eight, three and five. You continue with the ♣K, on which go the nine, four and queen. What do partner's two plays in clubs mean and what do you lead next?

7.5

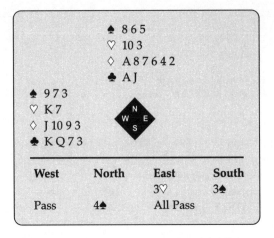

		♠ 8 6 5	
		♡ 10 3	
		◇ A 8 7 6 4 2	
		♣ A J	

♠ 9 7 3
♡ K 7
◇ J 10 9 3
♣ K Q 7 3

West	North	East	South
		3♡	3♠
Pass	4♠	All Pass	

You lead the ♡K, which wins when East plays the jack and South the five. What do you make of partner's ♡J and what card do you lead to the next trick?

7.6

	♠ A K Q J 5	
	♡ Q 8 4	
	◇ 8 6	
	♣ 10 6 2	

♠ 9 4 3 2
♡ 10 6 3
◇ Q 10 5 3
♣ A K

West	North	East	South
			1♡
Pass	1♠	Pass	2◇
Pass	4♡	All Pass	

Partner leads the ♣Q. What cards do you play at the first and second tricks? If the next card you see from partner is the ♣8 or the ♣9, what will you lead to the third trick?

Solutions

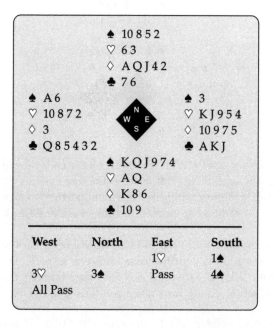

West	North	East	South
		1♡	1♠
3♡	3♠	Pass	4♠
All Pass			

Partner leads the ◇3 and declarer plays low from dummy. What do you play and why?

Since your side has bid and supported hearts, you expected a heart lead. One reason perhaps not to lead the suit is if partner has the ♡A. Even then it would be unlucky, given that you have opened 1♡, to find South with the ♡K. Can you see another reason for a diamond lead?

With nine cards in the suit between your hand and dummy, it is not hard to guess, especially as declarer's play of a low diamond from dummy makes it clear who has the king. The ◇3 must be a singleton. No doubt, partner intends to win an early round of trumps and put you in with a heart in the expectation of scoring a diamond ruff.

Fortunately, playing suit-preference signals, you can make sure this does not happen. Rather than making a pointless attempt to knock out the ◇K with the 'normal' play of the nine, play your lowest diamond, the five. This way partner, after coming in with the ♠A, will know to play a club rather than a heart. Of course, if you had strong hearts, and especially a quick entry in the suit, it would again be wrong to play the ◇9. You would play your highest diamond, the ten, to ask for a heart.

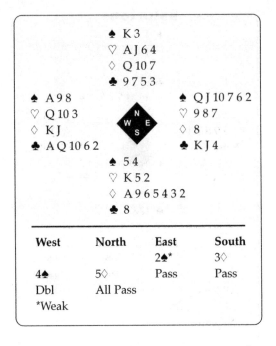

		♠ K 3	
		♡ A J 6 4	
		◊ Q 10 7	
		♣ 9 7 5 3	

West	East
♠ A 9 8	♠ Q J 10 7 6 2
♡ Q 10 3	♡ 9 8 7
◊ K J	◊ 8
♣ A Q 10 6 2	♣ K J 4

	♠ 5 4
	♡ K 5 2
	◊ A 9 6 5 4 3 2
	♣ 8

West	North	East	South
		2♠*	3◊
4♠	5◊	Pass	Pass
Dbl	All Pass		
*Weak			

You lead the ♠A, on which go the three, two and five. What meaning do you attribute to partner's ♠2 and what do you lead next?

Partner's opening bid and the spade holding in dummy make it clear that you cannot make any more tricks in the suit. Partner's length and strength in spades are both irrelevant. In this situation, in which neither an attitude nor a count signal would be of any use, partner should give you a suit-preference signal. With presumably a choice of six spades to play, partner has a wide range of cards available. This means the play of either the highest or the lowest of these conveys a strong message.

The ♠Q or, if South has this card, the ♠J, would ask for hearts, the higher-ranking of the unplayed side suits. Partner's actual choice of the ♠2 is the lowest spade missing and asks for the lower-ranking club suit. Accordingly, you should cash the ♣A and continue the suit.

Admittedly, there is some temptation to play the ♣A anyway. With your trumps as they are, it is the setting trick. Still, having doubled the final contract, you would like to make two club tricks if they were due. At the table, West missed the significance of the ♠2 and tried a second spade. Declarer cashed the ◊A and turned to hearts. With the finesse right and the suit 3-3, declarer was able to discard the ♣8 on the fourth round. The defenders took only two tricks: the ♠A and the ◊K.

```
                        ♠ K 8 3
                        ♡ J 10 6
                        ◇ K 6 3 2
                        ♣ Q 10 3
        ♠ 5                              ♠ J 7
        ♡ 9 8 7 3          N            ♡ K Q 4 2
        ◇ J 9 8 7 4     W     E         ◇ A Q
        ♣ A J 5            S            ♣ 9 7 6 4 2
                        ♠ A Q 10 9 6 4 2
                        ♡ A 5
                        ◇ 10 5
                        ♣ K 8
```

West	North	East	South
		1♣¹	1♠
Dbl²	2♠	Pass	4♠
All Pass			

¹May be short
²Negative

Partner leads the ♡8 and dummy covers with the ten. What card do you play and why?

There are three options here: to duck if you think South's ♡A is bare, to play a normal ♡Q to suggest you might have the ♡K as well, or to play the ♡K, ostensibly denying the ♡Q.

Since it seems that partner was too weak to bid 2♡ over 1♠, the ♡A just might be singleton. Even so, it would be an extreme view to play for that. Your real choice lies between playing the ♡Q and the ♡K.

To reach the right decision you need to ask yourself what suit you want led if partner comes in with the ♣K or the ♣A. Clearly, the answer is diamonds, not hearts. Therefore, to discourage hearts you should play the ♡K, pretending that you do not hold the ♡Q. This will leave partner little choice but to try a diamond after coming in with the ♣A.

Note that it would be different if you had one more diamond and one fewer heart (i.e. ♡K-Q-2 and ◇A-Q-5). In that case, you could not be sure you want a diamond switch. If the lead is from 9-8-7-x and West leads a heart again, your side could score two hearts and it would not matter if South held a singleton diamond. Then you would play the ♡Q.

More on Following to Partner's Lead   99

7.4

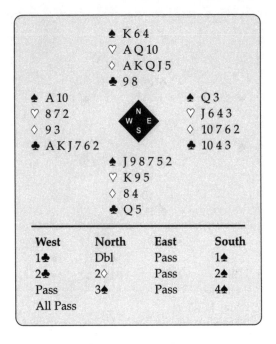

	♠ K 6 4	
	♡ A Q 10	
	◇ A K Q J 5	
	♣ 9 8	

♠ A 10		♠ Q 3
♡ 8 7 2		♡ J 6 4 3
◇ 9 3		◇ 10 7 6 2
♣ A K J 7 6 2		♣ 10 4 3

	♠ J 9 8 7 5 2	
	♡ K 9 5	
	◇ 8 4	
	♣ Q 5	

West	North	East	South
1♣	Dbl	Pass	1♠
2♣	2◇	Pass	2♠
Pass	3♠	Pass	4♠
All Pass			

Your lead of the ♣A collects the eight, three and five. You continue with the ♣K, on which go the nine, four and queen. What do partner's two plays in clubs mean and what do you lead next?

On the first round, it is reasonable to read the ♣3, the lowest club out, as indicating an odd number of clubs. In a trump contract, and with the doubleton club in dummy, you would hardly want an attitude signal to tell you who holds the ♣Q. This means partner started with 10-4-3.

Having played the ♣3 on the first round, partner had a choice of two cards to play. Other things being equal, the higher of these would ask for the higher red suit, hearts, while the lower asks for the lower red suit, diamonds. However, everyone can see East cannot really want a diamond. Dummy's holding is solid and, as South failed to raise the suit, there is no hope of a ruff. So, does the ♣4 tell you nothing?

On the contrary, you have a strong negative inference. East, if holding the ♡K, would surely play the ♣10 to ask for hearts. Therefore, you must place South with the ♡K. In this case, the only way to beat the contract is with a second trump trick. Play a third round of clubs and a fourth after you take the first round of trumps with the ace. This allows partner to score the ♠Q as the setting trick.

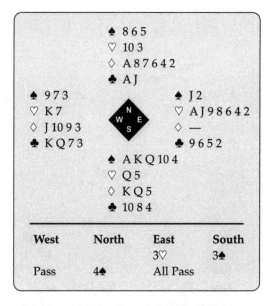

West	North	East	South
		3♡	3♠
Pass	4♠	All Pass	

You lead the ♡K, which wins when East plays the jack and South the five. What do you make of partner's ♡J and what card do you lead to the next trick?

The bidding tells you that partner has a lot of hearts, probably seven if you play weak twos, and therefore has a wide choice of cards to play. This means, even if you could not see the ♡10 in dummy, that the ♡J is an unusually high card to play, not a normal length or attitude signal.

An unusually high or low card in this situation is a suit-preference signal. The jack is a high card and asks for the higher minor, diamonds. Given that you can see ten cards in the suit between your hand and dummy, it is not hard to see why this might be the case. East, surely, holds a void in diamonds.

Assuming that a diamond switch will be giving a ruff, it is your turn to give a suit-preference signal. Yes, both defenders can give one on the same deal! From partner's point of view, it will be attractive to return a heart in the hope you started with K-Q alone or a singleton heart. On your actual hand the last thing you want is to take the risk that partner will underlead the ♡A to your hypothetical ♡Q. To ensure this does not happen, lead your lowest diamond, the three. Partner, after ruffing, will now know to lead a club. (Cashing the ♡A before this will not cost). Declarer will be unable to draw trumps ending in dummy and, with the diamonds blocked, will have to lose a club trick to go one down.

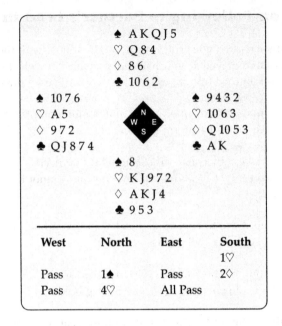

	♠ A K Q J 5	
	♡ Q 8 4	
	◇ 8 6	
	♣ 10 6 2	
♠ 10 7 6		♠ 9 4 3 2
♡ A 5		♡ 10 6 3
◇ 9 7 2		◇ Q 10 5 3
♣ Q J 8 7 4		♣ A K
	♠ 8	
	♡ K J 9 7 2	
	◇ A K J 4	
	♣ 9 5 3	

West	North	East	South
			1♡
Pass	1♠	Pass	2◇
Pass	4♡	All Pass	

Partner leads the ♣Q. What cards do you play at the first and second tricks? If the next card you see from partner is the ♣8 or the ♣9, what will you lead to the third trick?

Although the usual rule is to play the lower of touching cards, you will have gathered by now that this chapter is packed full of exceptional cases. Yes, with the ace-king and others you would play the king. With ace-king doubleton, however, you should play the ace before the king. This reverse order generally means that you have A-K alone.

Given that your play in clubs will show your doubleton, partner will know you will have to switch. This gives us a suit-preference position on the second round of clubs. With some values in diamonds partner will play a low club. How do you read a high club, which the ♣9 would be and the ♣8, is unless the lead was from precisely Q-J-9-8?

It cannot seriously ask for a spade. Dummy's holding in spades is very strong and South's inability to raise the suit (and ability to bid both red suits and follow to two clubs) rules out a spade ruff. Playing the ♣8 (or ♣9) simply denies interest in diamonds. Trusting this, you try a trump at the third trick. Sure enough, partner wins with the ace and cashes the ♣J for the setting trick. Of course, the contract would make if you led a diamond at the third trick. Declarer would go up with the ace and discard a club on the second round of spades.

More on Following to Partner's Lead in Brief

- If partner returns your suit, you normally follow with the card you would have played if you had led it again yourself, for example your bottom card from five cards and upwards with three low.

- You can make an exception to this if it is more important to deceive declarer than it is to inform partner.

- You overtake rather than give a signal if you need to gain the lead to take control, or to play a suit that partner cannot lead or cannot lead profitably.

- You do not have to encourage just because you like the suit led. If you are keen for a switch, discourage.

- Unless you are short in the suit and need to unblock, overtaking partner's lead generally suggests a strong holding.

- Play the higher of touching cards in third seat with something like A-K alone or to convey a special message such as a void in another suit.

- Play the higher card also if you want to encourage partner to switch, or to deceive declarer.

- Having shown count or attitude on partner's first lead, you give a suit-preference signal on the second round. A high card asks for the higher-ranking side-suit (you exclude the one being played) and a very low card asks for the lower ranking.

- In giving a suit-preference signal, the middle card, if you have one, is usually neutral between the other two side suits.

- When you have a very long suit, you can give a suit-preference signal on the first round with a very high or very low card.

- If partner leads a singleton, or it is clear there is no future in the suit led, again you can give suit-preference on the first round.

Chapter 8
More on Following
to an Opponent's Lead

You will recall that, in giving a signal in a suit led by an opponent, you normally show your length, playing a high spot card with an even number and your lowest card with an odd number. If you have a choice, what do you on the second round? You can probably guess the answer from the previous chapter. You give a suit-preference signal. On most deals, you can exclude one suit from the equation, either because it is the trump suit or because it is dummy's main suit. In this case, you express preference between the other two suits.

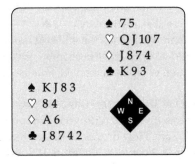

```
                       ♠ 7 5
                       ♡ Q J 10 7
                       ◊ J 8 7 4
                       ♣ K 9 3
        ♠ K J 8 3
        ♡ 8 4              N
        ◊ A 6          W       E
        ♣ J 8 7 4 2        S
```

South plays in 3NT on the sequence 1◊ – 1♡ – 2NT(18-19) – 3NT. You lead the ♣4, East plays the queen and the ace wins. Declarer plays the ◊3 to the jack, East following with the ◊2, and one back to the king, on which East plays the five. What do you do?

Clearly, partner began with ◊9-5-2 or ◊10-5-2 because the ◊2 on the first round showed an odd number. It is also clear that the ◊5 was the lower of partner's remaining diamonds. Given dummy's strong hearts, partner should be giving preference between the black suits. The ◊5 should indicate something in clubs, the ten when the position of the other high clubs is marked. So you continue with a low club. You are not worried about a blockage as a spade switch would suit you fine.

What would you do if partner played the ◊10 on the second round? You would take that as showing spade values, ideally the ace or maybe the queen, and switch to a low spade.

You may recall from Chapter 2 that with four cards you normally play your second-highest card on the first round of an opposing lead. If your four cards are all low, you have a wide choice on the second round. Suppose you have 9-8-3-2 and have played the eight. Your normal card on the second round is the third highest, the three. This leaves the nine and the two free for sending a suit-preference signal.

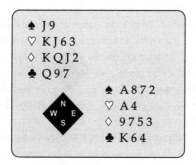

South plays in 3NT on the auction 1NT – 2♣ – 2◇ – 3NT. 1NT is weak (12-14) and 2♣ Stayman. West leads the ♠5 and your ace wins. You return the ♠2 and West follows with the three under the king. Declarer plays low to the ◇K, on which you play the seven, and leads the ◇2 off dummy.

Partner may be about to show out on this trick and will be keen to know whether to keep hearts or clubs. With your ♡A, you know that a heart discard is completely safe. How do you signal for hearts? On this deal the spade layout is clear to everyone. Given that South denied holding a four-card major, your return of the ♠2 must have been from four rather than a doubleton. You can therefore exclude spades from the suit-preference options and use a high diamond, the nine, to show the ♡A (or at any rate a stopper in the suit).

```
          ♠ Q 10 6 5 3
          ♡ Q 9 7 2
          ◇ 8
          ♣ 10 8 2
```

If this is partner's hand, it is vital that you get the message across. Even one club discard could allow declarer to run the queen to pick up the suit. Of course, if you had the ♣A instead of the ♡A, it would be equally vital to play the ◇3 on the second round. In that case, partner would need to hang on to four hearts to stop that suit from running.

In Chapter 3, we touched on the possibility of holding up a stopper to wait for a discard from partner. In a similar vein, you might hold up to wait for a suit-preference signal.

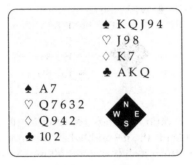

North opens 1♠ and raises South's 1NT response to game. You lead the ♡3, which goes to the nine, ten and ace. What are your thoughts when the ♠10 appears for the next trick?

No matter when you take your ♠A, declarer will have four spade tricks. These, together with three clubs, the ♡A and either the ◇A or the ♡K will suffice for game. After taking your ♠A, you will need to win the next four tricks. The simplest chance for this is that the hearts are now running. The alternative, if South holds the ♡K, is to find partner with ◇A-J-x-(x). Given that you have the diamonds stopped, rather than guess now, let the ♠10 win the first round of spades.

East plays the ♠6, suggesting a four-card holding as you would guess from the bidding. South leads a second spade, the five, and now let us say East drops the eight. This is a high card, asking for the highest suit for which it would be sensible to ask. Therefore, you continue with a low heart, hoping partner has a low heart to go with the king.

How would you read the ♠2 on the second round? In view of dummy's club holding, this could not be asking for a club. It must be indicating values in diamonds, so you would switch to the ◇ 2.

In Chapter 2, I said that you do not give the same length signals in the trump suit as in the side suits. This is because it often helps declarer more than anyone else to know how the trumps are breaking. In any case, the defenders may well have an idea of declarer's trump length from the bidding. The traditional meaning of a high-low in trumps is to show a third trump and the ability to ruff. Yes, you have read that right. You only peter or echo in trumps with an odd number of trumps.

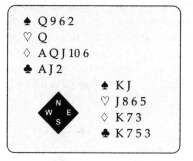

North opens 1◊ and South responds 1♠. After North raises to 3♠, South goes on to 4♠. West leads the ♣9 and, when dummy plays low, you win with the king. You return a club and all follow. Declarer now plays the ace of trumps and another to the nine and king.

Although South must hold the missing clubs, it is less clear whether West has a trump left with which to ruff. If you lead a club and South has the remaining trumps but not the ♡A, the ♡Q will go away on the fourth club. It would be equally fatal to lead a heart if South has the ♡A and your side needed a club ruff. This is where the trump echo comes in so useful. With three trumps West plays high-low (usually with the middle and bottom cards, say the eight and five from 10-8-5). If this happens, you know to play a third club. With only a doubleton trump, West does not play high-low and you will have to try a heart.

The next layout is another good one for a trump echo:

If declarer draws two rounds of trumps (hearts) with the ace and king before leading another suit, it usually means one of two things. One is that the defenders have no more trumps. The second is that there is a master trump out. Clearly, knowing whether South has six trump tricks (with A-K-Q-J-10-3) or four might help East. Assuming nobody can think a ruff is on, West plays high-low with Q-x-x and upwards with x-x.

Another time for the trump echo with three (or five) trumps is when a forcing game might be on. A failure to echo then suggests four trumps.

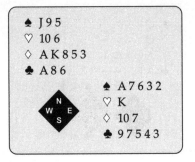

```
        ♠ J 9 5
        ♡ 10 6
        ◇ A K 8 5 3
        ♣ A 8 6
                        ♠ A 7 6 3 2
                        ♡ K
              N         ◇ 10 7
           W     E      ♣ 9 7 5 4 3
              S
```

North opens a 12-14 1NT and South jumps to 4♡. West leads the ♣4 and
your ♠A fells the king. You return the ♠3 (your original fourth best). After
ruffing, South leads the ♡3, which goes two, ten, king.

There are two main chances here. The first is to keep playing spades in
the hope that South, with only six hearts, loses control. The second is to
try a club in the hope West has K-J or even K-Q. Since the ♡2 is clearly
low, and trusting that West would have begun a high-low with an odd
number of trumps (three), you persevere with spades. West, who began
with ♡A-7-5-2, will play a fourth spade after taking the ♡A.

Test Yourself

8.1

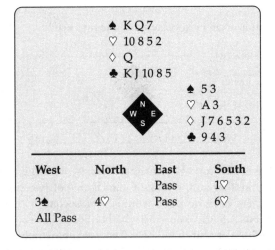

```
        ♠ K Q 7
        ♡ 10 8 5 2
        ◇ Q
        ♣ K J 10 8 5
                        ♠ 5 3
                        ♡ A 3
              N         ◇ J 7 6 5 3 2
           W     E      ♣ 9 4 3
              S
```

West	North	East	South
		Pass	1♡
3♠	4♡	Pass	6♡
All Pass			

Partner leads the ♠J and the ace wins. After declarer leads the ◇9 to the
queen, the ♠K comes followed by the ♠Q. (West played the ♠6 on the
second spade while South threw a club.) What do you do?

8.2

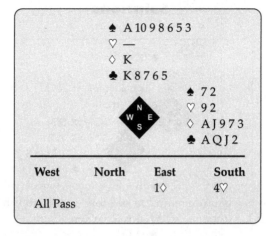

	♠ A 10 9 8 6 5 3		
	♡ —		
	◇ K		
	♣ K 8 7 6 5		

		♠ 7 2
		♡ 9 2
		◇ A J 9 7 3
		♣ A Q J 2

West	North	East	South
		1◇	4♡
All Pass			

Partner leads the ♠K to dummy's ace. Having discarded a club on this, declarer ruffs a spade (West plays the four) before laying down the ace and king of trumps. Partner plays the ♡6 followed by the ♡3 on these trumps and the ◇5 on South's next lead of the ◇6. Do you capture the ◇K with the ace and, if you do, what do you lead next?

8.3

	♠ K J 10 5		
	♡ K Q 8 3		
	◇ K 8 3		
	♣ Q 4		

♠ A 6	
♡ J 9 5	
◇ J 9 5 4	
♣ K J 10 5	

West	North	East	South
			1♣
Pass	1♡	Pass	1NT*
Pass	3NT	All Pass	
*12-14			

You lead the ◇4 and East's ten loses to the queen. At the second trick declarer leads a low spade. Can you see any purpose in ducking? What will you do if partner plays the ♠8 on the first round and the ♠2 on the next? What would you do if the ♠9 came after the eight?

Solutions

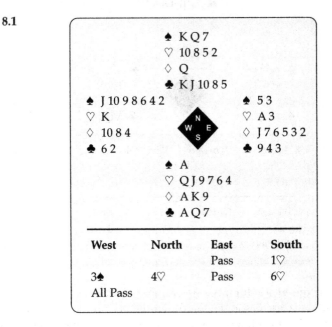

West	North	East	South
		Pass	1♡
3♠	4♡	Pass	6♡
All Pass			

Partner leads the ♠J and the ace wins on your left. Declarer leads the ◇9 to the queen and next comes the ♠K followed by the ♠Q. West, if you want to know, played the ♠6 on the second round of spades while South threw a club. What do you do?

The temptation here is to ruff the third round of spades in order to stop declarer from discarding a losing club. If this is the right thing to do, West has the ♣A. Can you see any reason why this cannot be so?

There are two good reasons for placing the ♣A with South. For one thing, with two aces missing South might have used Blackwood on the way to 6♡. A better one is the play in spades. Holding the ♣A it would be natural to play the ♠2 on the second round as a suit-preference signal for clubs. What has actually happened is that West has carefully played a neutral ♠6. This means South has the ♣A and ruffing is pointless. As the cards lie, it would be fatal to ruff with the ♡3 and be overruffed. Then your ace of trumps would fall with partner's king.

Note that it would not help declarer to cross to the ♣K rather than the ◇Q (and throw the ◇9). In that case, West's middling ♠6 would tell you South has the ◇A and again you should do the right thing.

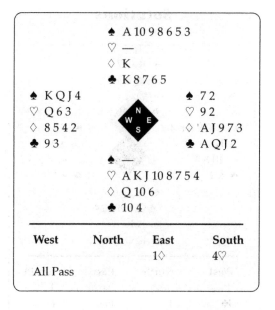

West	North	East	South
		1◇	4♡
All Pass			

Partner leads the ♠K to dummy's ace. Having discarded a club on this, declarer ruffs a spade before laying down the ace and king of trumps. Partner plays the ♠4 followed by the ♡6 and ♡3 and then the ◇5 on South's next lead of the ◇6. Do you capture the ◇K with the ace and, if you do, what do you lead next?

The natural play, in the absence of any signals, is to win with the ◇A and return a diamond. This will be safe if partner has either the ◇Q or the ◇10. To stand a chance of defeating the contract if instead South has these two cards, you will need to let the ◇K win. If you gain the lead, you will, after cashing the ♣A, have no safe exit. A club would concede a trick to dummy, while a diamond would give declarer a free finesse.

It all seems to depend upon whether you can count on partner for a trump trick. If you can, you do not need three diamond tricks to go with the ♣A. There are two clues here, both pointing in the same direction. Firstly, with a solid eight-card trump suit declarer might have drawn a third round of trumps. More importantly, you would not expect West to play high-low with the ♡6 and ♡3 holding three low trumps. This echo or peter, whichever you wish to call it, should show the ♡Q.

I might mention that partner could have played the ♠Q on the second round of spades as a suit-preference signal for diamonds if holding the ◇Q. The other signal West did make was the ◇5 on the first round, in this case second highest from 8-5-4-2.

```
                    ♠ K J 10 5
                    ♡ K Q 8 3
                    ◇ K 8 3
                    ♣ Q 4
   ♠ A 6                              ♠ 9 8 3 2
   ♡ J 9 5           N                ♡ 10 7 6 4
   ◇ J 9 5 4      W     E             ◇ 10 7 2
   ♣ K J 10 5        S                ♣ A 6
                    ♠ Q 7 4
                    ♡ A 2
                    ◇ A Q 6
                    ♣ 9 8 7 3 2
```

West	North	East	South
			1♣
Pass	1♡	Pass	1NT*
Pass	3NT	All Pass	
*12-14			

You lead the ◇4 and East's ten loses to the queen. At the second trick declarer leads a low spade. Can you see any purpose in ducking?

Since you do not know what to do next, it looks right to duck the first spade. There is a vague chance that East has the ♠Q and, with your holdings in the minors, no danger that declarer can run nine fast tricks.

What will you do if partner plays the ♠8 on the first round and the ♠2 on the next? You read the ♠8 as a high card, from a four-card suit no doubt. What do you make of the ♠2 on the second round? This is a low card, not a normal third highest, and must mean something.

Counting points, you place South with exactly two of the three missing aces. So, whether or not you exclude hearts from the equation, the low suit for which East must be asking is clubs. Therefore, you should lead the ♣5. As the cards lie, this allows you to cash four club tricks.

What would you do if the ♣9 came after the eight? It is not so clear-cut which red ace East has. Dummy's hearts are not so good as to rule out a heart switch. This means it might be one of those rare times when, from 9-8-3-2, the ♣9 would ask for a heart, the ♣3 for a diamond and the ♣2 for a club. Luckily, it would not matter. You would lead the ◇J next, which may pick up dummy's king and will certainly be safe.

More on Following to an Opponent's Lead in Brief

- Once you have given a count signal, your play on the second round normally indicates suit-preference.

- Usually there is a trump suit, or one suit you cannot possibly want, and you express preference between the remaining two.

- As normal, a high card in context asks for the higher-ranking suit and a low card asks for the lower ranking.

- A middle card indicates no preference or, in the unusual case that three suits remain in the picture, values in the middle suit.

- A high-low in trumps indicates an odd number of trumps, but you only use this signal on special occasions.

- The trump echo applies especially to say that you have a trump left with which you can ruff something.

- You can also use the trump echo to say you have a trump winner or help partner judge whether a forcing game is possible.

- Take care as always only to signal with a card you can spare.

Chapter 9
More on Discarding

W hen we discussed discards before, the main objective was to show the location of your strength. Suppose you have few or no cards of value and your objective is to reveal where declarer's losers are. What should you do then? Often voiding yourself in a suit provides the answer. If all the cards in a suit are gone or accounted for, partner can work out that there is no longer a need to guard the suit.

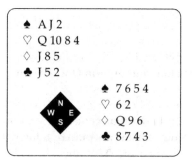

♠ A J 2
♡ Q 10 8 4
◇ J 8 5
♣ J 5 2

♠ 7 6 5 4
♡ 6 2
◇ Q 9 6
♣ 8 7 4 3

South opens 1♠, West overcalls 2♡, North raises to 2♠ and South jumps to 4♠. West leads the ◇A, on which you encourage with the nine. Then, when all follow to partner's ◇K and your ◇Q, your side has won the first three tricks. When you switch to the ♡6, declarer wins with the ace and plays five rounds of trumps. Partner, who is void, throws four hearts and a diamond. What should you discard?

For the play to matter South must have the ♣A-K and West the queen. (If West has the ♣A or ♣K, the contract will fail, while if South has the ♣A-K-Q, there is no hope). In this case, declarer has nine top tricks and, on the next round of trumps, partner will need to judge whether South started with ♡A-x and ♣A-K doubleton, or a singleton ♡A and ♣A-K-x. Since your switch to the ♡6 is consistent with either a singleton ♡6 or your actual holding, you should clarify the position by discarding the ♡2.

Another way to help partner read the distribution is to show count with a discard. This applies if it is already clear whether you like the suit you throw, normally because of weakness but possibly because of strength.

```
                    ♠ K 7 5
                    ♡ Q 3
                    ◇ K Q J 10 3
                    ♣ Q 10 4
                                    ♠ 9 6 3
                                    ♡ 10 7
                          N         ◇ 9 8 7 5 2
                       W     E      ♣ K 7 3
                          S

    West        North       East        South
                                        1♠
    2♡          3◇          Pass        3♠
    Pass        4♠          All Pass
```

West leads the ♡A followed by the ♡K and ♡9. You play high-low with the ten and seven before dummy ruffs the ♡9 with the ♠K.

Can you see partner's problem on this deal? It is judging when to take the ◇A. How do you know that South does not have this card? Even without suit-preference signals, it would be a fair bet that West would, if able to do so, have cashed the ♣A rather than playing the third heart. This means South has the ♣A. This tells you there is little hope unless partner has one of the other aces. If you recall Chapter 4, you will have even better reason to place partner with the ◇A. If South has the ♡J, the ♡9 is the highest heart West could lead on the third round. A classic suit-preference signal is with leading a suit that you might ruff.

With your actual hand, you have a shrewd idea that West needs to take the ◇A on the first round. The best way to achieve this is to throw the ◇2, showing an odd number, five in this instance. This shows an odd number rather than a lack of interest in the suit because the latter is already obvious from the look of dummy. What would you do if instead you had the hand below? Then you would discard the ◇7, following the usual rule of playing second highest from a four-card holding.

```
                    ♠ 9 6 3
                    ♡ 10 7
                    ◇ 9 7 5 2
                    ♣ K 8 7 3
```

Talking about suit-preference signals, what might be the meaning of discard from a suit in which both your attitude and your length are clear? Suppose here that diamonds are trumps and West leads the ♠10. You, East, win with the ace and return the queen, which South ruffs. West now knows your spade holding, which means that a spade discard cannot say something about your spades. Instead, it shows suit preference. The ♠8 would ask for or express interest in hearts, while the ♠2 would do the same for clubs. The ♠5 and ♠6 are neutral cards to discard.

Most of the time we have talked about how playing the right card saves partner a guess. You must not forget that declarer, who will be tuning in to your signals, may be the one with a guess. On this layout, as East, you need to duck smoothly when declarer leads a spade to the king so that there is a guess on the next round whether to play to the queen or finesse the ten. The effect of ducking smoothly, however, will be lost if you have discarded the ♠9 to signal your strength in spades.

Likewise, if declarer's sole objective on this layout is to avoid the loss of two spades , it will be a matter of judging whether to play low to the king or to finesse the jack. Again, unless you have a tricky reputation, you should not discard an encouraging ♠8 early in the play. Either discard a different suit (because it would obviously be unattractive to discard from Q-x-x) or, if you must throw a spade, discard a lower card.

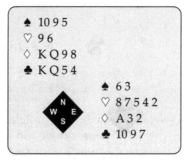

♠ 10 9 5
♡ 9 6
◇ K Q 9 8
♣ K Q 5 4

♠ 6 3
♡ 8 7 5 4 2
◇ A 3 2
♣ 10 9 7

After South has opened 1♡ and West has doubled for take-out, South plays in 4♡. West leads the ♠A followed by the ♠Q and ♠K. What do you think you should be doing?

So long as South has a diamond, you can see how to set the contract. Unfortunately, partner may not read either the ◇3 as encouraging or the ♣7 as discouraging. Partner will surely play a fourth round of spades expecting you to overruff dummy. This could be a disaster. If South's shape is 4-6-1-2, your ◇A will never score. Happily, there is an easy solution. Ruff the ♠K and cash the ◇A.

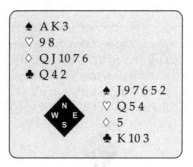

♠ A K 3
♡ 9 8
◇ Q J 10 7 6
♣ Q 4 2

♠ J 9 7 6 5 2
♡ Q 5 4
◇ 5
♣ K 10 3

After a simple 1NT(15-17) – 3NT, West leads the ♡6 to the eight, queen and ace. Having crossed to dummy with a spade, declarer runs the ◇Q, which holds. What do you discard on the second diamond?

The strength of the dummy suggests that the only way to defeat this contract is to find partner with a diamond stopper and running hearts. The position may be less clear to West if South has the ♡J left. In that case, it might be right to try to put you in with a club for a heart through South's possible ♡J-x. To clarify the position, you discard the card you would have returned, the ♡5. Particularly since you would not rush to throw your only remaining heart, partner should read the position.

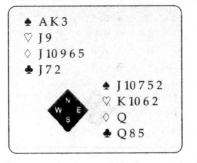

The bidding (and the 1NT range) are the same as before. **Partner leads** the ♡5, which goes to the jack, king and ace. Crossing to the ♠A, declarer leads the ◊J off dummy, which goes to the queen, king and **seven. When** West's ace wins the next diamond, you must discard.

You can go one better now. If the ♡5 was fourth highest, **South started** with only one heart higher than the five. You have already **seen this, the** ace. If you throw the ♡10, West will be sure that the suit is **running.**

Test Yourself

9.1

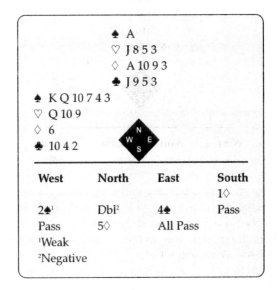

	♠ A		
	♡ J 8 5 3		
	◊ A 10 9 3		
	♣ J 9 5 3		

♠ K Q 10 7 4 3
♡ Q 10 9
◊ 6
♣ 10 4 2

West	North	East	South
			1◊
2♠[1]	Dbl[2]	4♠	Pass
Pass	5◊	All Pass	

[1] Weak
[2] Negative

You lead the ♠K to the ace, six and jack. Declarer leads **the ◊A from** dummy, on which partner drops the jack, and leads a second **round to** partner's king. What do you discard?

9.2

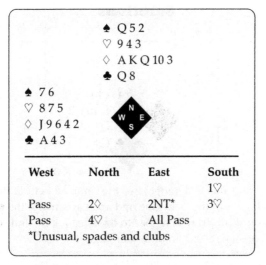

	♠ Q 5 2
	♡ 9 4 3
	◊ A K Q 10 3
	♣ Q 8

♠ 7 6
♡ 8 7 5
◊ J 9 6 4 2
♣ A 4 3

West	North	East	South
			1♡
Pass	2◊	2NT*	3♡
Pass	4♡	All Pass	

*Unusual, spades and clubs

You lead the ♠7, which goes to the two, ten and eight. Partner then cashes the ♠A and continues with the ♠K, South following all the way. What do you play on this third round of spades?

9.3

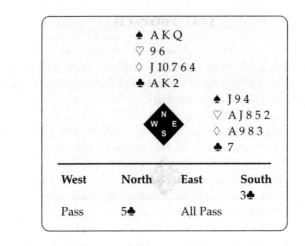

	♠ A K Q
	♡ 9 6
	◊ J 10 7 6 4
	♣ A K 2

♠ J 9 4
♡ A J 8 5 2
◊ A 9 8 3
♣ 7

West	North	East	South
			3♣
Pass	5♣	All Pass	

Partner leads the ♡4 and your ace drops South's queen. You return the ♡5, which is ruffed. A club goes to the ace and now you need to find a discard on the ♣K. What will it be?

Solutions

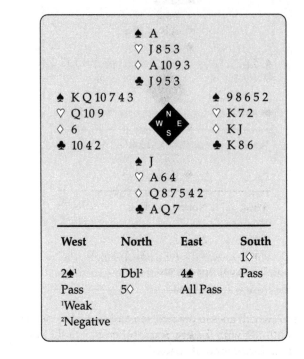

	♠ A		
	♡ J 8 5 3		
	◇ A 10 9 3		
	♣ J 9 5 3		

♠ K Q 10 7 4 3		♠ 9 8 6 5 2
♡ Q 10 9		♡ K 7 2
◇ 6		◇ K J
♣ 10 4 2		♣ K 8 6

	♠ J		
	♡ A 6 4		
	◇ Q 8 7 5 4 2		
	♣ A Q 7		

West	North	East	South
			1◇
2♠¹	Dbl²	4♠	Pass
Pass	5◇	All Pass	

¹Weak
²Negative

You lead the ♠K to the ace, six and jack. Declarer leads the ◇A from dummy, on which partner drops the jack, and then leads a second round to partner's king. What do you discard?

Partner's ♣6 on the first trick looks neither high nor low. Since, with no spade winners possible your way, this is a suit-preference situation, it looks like partner has equal holdings in hearts and clubs, perhaps the king in both. From the bidding (and declarer's failure to ruff a spade in dummy), partner will be able to work out not to lead a second spade but not whether a heart is safer than a club.

You can ill afford to discard an encouraging ♡10. Declarer might hop up with the ♡A on the first round and throw you in with the ♡Q. A lead from the ♣10 might then cost a trick. Equally, you cannot spare the ♣2. Declarer might run the ♣J off dummy and later drop your ten. It makes sense to discard a spade and, with your length and strength in the suit already clear, you can give a suit-preference signal in doing so. Hearts are higher than clubs and the ♠10 is probably high enough to get the job done. Playing the ♠Q would be better with some partners!

9.2

```
                    ♠ Q 5 2
                    ♡ 9 4 3
                    ◇ A K Q 10 3
                    ♣ Q 8
    ♠ 7 6                          ♠ A K J 10 3
    ♡ 8 7 5          N             ♡ 6
    ◇ J 9 6 4 2   W     E          ◇ 8
    ♣ A 4 3          S             ♣ J 9 7 6 5 2
                    ♠ 9 8 4
                    ♡ A K Q J 10 2
                    ◇ 7 5
                    ♣ K 10
```

West	North	East	South
			1♡
Pass	2◇	2NT*	3♡
Pass	4♡	All Pass	

*Unusual, spades and clubs

You lead the ♣7, which goes to the two, ten and eight. Partner then cashes the ♠A and continues with the ♠K, South following all the way. What do you play on this third round of spades?

Again, it does not figure to do you much good if you make an attitude discard. The ♣4 will probably be too small to look encouraging and, although you can easily discourage diamonds, playing the ◇2 hardly asks for a club. If you throw either of these cards, you can guess what will happen. East will play a fourth spade and feel bitterly disappointed when declarer discards a club and you cannot produce a heart higher than dummy's nine.

You cannot complain about this. If your trumps were J-x-x, Q-x or, less likely, 10-x-x-x, a fourth round of spades would promote your holding into a trick. If you did not have the ♣A, that would be the setting trick. Fortunately, there is a simple solution. Ruff the third round of spades and cash your ♣A.

Incidentally, if you had a trump holding that you wanted to promote and an observant but unimaginative partner, you might discard the ◇J. As is customary, an unusual card asks for an unusual play, a category into which giving a ruff-and-discard generally falls.

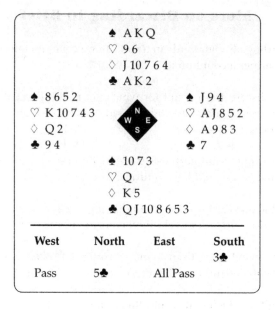

West	North	East	South
			3♣
Pass	5♣	All Pass	

Partner leads the ♡4 and your ace drops South's queen. You return the ♡5, which is ruffed. A club goes to the ace and now you need to find a discard on the ♣K. What will it be?

Assuming South has a sane 3♣ opener, partner will not have a trump winner. To beat the contract you will therefore need to score two tricks in diamonds. If you reckon that West would have led a diamond from the king-queen in preference to a heart from the king-ten, you can place South with the ◇K or the ◇Q. In the latter case, your side has two top winners and it might sound like a nice idea to discard the ◇9 to share the news. Unfortunately, revealing that you have the ◇A will not be very smart if South has the ◇K and presumably a guess in the suit.

There are certainly two safe discards here, the ♠4 and the ♡8. Then all you have to do is duck smoothly when the ◇J comes off dummy. There will be every chance that declarer, with K-x, will let the ◇J run. Even when there is no particular reason to do so, players tend to play for split aces, putting West with the ◇A just because you had the ♡A.

By the way, did you work out why I suggested discarding the ♡8 and not the ♡2? Since South has shown out of hearts, any heart discard you make will have suit-preference overtones. If you want to carry the pretence of not holding the ◇A to its logical conclusion, you do not want to part with your lowest remaining heart.

More on Discarding in Brief

- Discarding all your cards in a suit often proves an effective way to give partner a count on it.

- If you discard from a suit for which your attitude is already clear, give a count signal, low with an odd number or high with an even number.

- In discarding a suit partner led originally, you normally discard the card that you would have returned.

- With the one card needed to solidify partner's suit, discard it if it is safe to do so in order to clarify the position.

- Do not signal strength in a suit if you think declarer has a guess in it and will benefit from the information more than partner.

- In a suit in which both your attitude and your length are clear, any discard is a suit-preference signal.

- In that situation, remember not to throw your lowest card unless you want partner to place you with values in a low-ranking suit.

- With a trump to spare and a winner to cash, it may be better to ruff partner's winner than to make an ambiguous discard.

Chapter 10
More on Continuations and Returns

Y ou may recall that the usual rule for returning partner's suit is to lead your original fourth best from a long suit. Sometimes you can tell this will not be a good idea and return a higher card instead.

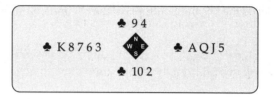

Suppose you are East, defending a no-trump contract, and win the first club with the ace. If you return the ♣5, you block the suit. Unless West has a side entry, your side scores four club tricks instead of five.

```
              ♠ —
              ♡ A Q 6 4
              ♢ 5 3 2
              ♣ Q J 10 8 5 3
                                ♠ K 10 7 5
                                ♡ K J 9 2
                                ♢ Q J 7
                                ♣ 9 2
```

South, who has shown a 15-17 1NT with a four-card spade suit, plays in 3NT. West leads the ♠6 and your king wins. What do you return?

If as seems likely, West has the ♠A, you can place South with A-K of both minors in order to have at least 15 points. In this case, you surely need to run five spade tricks to defeat the contract. A 'normal' return of the ♠5 will work if South has J-8-x-x but not do so well against Q-8-x-x. In the latter case, West will take the ♠8 with the nine but be unable to put you back in to lead through South's Q-x. You do better to return the ♠10. This gives you five spade tricks if West has A-J-9-x-x or A-Q-9-x-x.

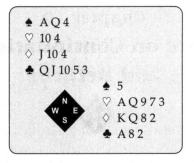

You open 1♡ in third seat, South overcalls 1NT and North raises this to 3NT. West leads the ♡5 and South plays the ♡8 under your ace.

There are only 15 points missing and you can be sure where they all are. Fortunately, it will not be so clear to declarer that your partner has a Yarborough. Does this give you any ideas?

If the ♡8 is a true card, West started with 6-5-2, which gives you a chance. Declarer cannot, if you are careful, tell that West has not led from Q-6-5, or Q-7-5, or Q-9-5. On those layouts, it would be right to rise with the king on the second round to block the hearts. So, rather than a revealing ♡7, try returning a deceptive ♡3. This may not work as some lead low from the likes of 9-6-5 in a suit bid but not supported. Still, it is worth a try.

After the ♢7 goes to the four, ace and five, it will be normal, if you return the suit, to lead the six to make the layout as clear as you can. On occasion, however, you will wish to fool declarer. If West has bid the suit, the ♢2 will look like a doubleton and declarer may waste a trump, possibly a high one, ruffing the third round in dummy.

There could also be a deceptive gain if West has not bid the suit. In this case, the return of the two may make it look like the diamonds are 4-4. How can that help, you ask? Well, perhaps you have Q-x-x of trumps. If declarer thinks you are short in diamonds, it will be attractive to finesse you for the trump queen. If, instead, it looks like diamonds are 4-4, it may be more natural to try to drop it.

```
                    ♠ 10 2
                    ♡ A K 3
                    ♦ K Q J
                    ♣ 9 8 4 3 2
                                    ♠ Q J 3
              N                     ♡ Q 10 4
           W     E                  ♦ A 4
              S                     ♣ A 10 7 6 5

    West       North      East       South
               1♣         Pass       1♠
    Pass       1NT        Pass       4♠
    All Pass
```

West leads the ♣J, clearly a singleton, and you win. What do you return?

With the ◇A re-entry, it seems clear to return your lowest club, the five, to ask for the low-ranking diamond suit. Alas, when you come back in and try a third round of clubs, what do you think will happen? Declarer, who is likely to have seven spades, will ruff and West will discard. With the trump position marked, declarer will cross to dummy twice in the red suits to take two finesses and pick up the trumps without loss.

A better bet is to return the ♣7, asking for a heart. Declarer cannot tell from the bidding that you have the ◇A and this could be (and in the sense that you hold the ♡Q is) a genuine signal. The difference now is that declarer, with ♠A-K-8-7-6-5-4, will surely play trumps from the top.

I should mention that you could make the deceptive plays on this deal and at the top of the previous page because you had all the defensive strength. With practically no values, partner will not mind being fooled.

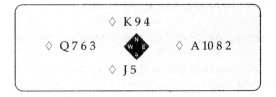

```
                    ◇ K 9 4
                          N
    ◇ Q 7 6 3        W          E     ◇ A 10 8 2
                          S
                    ◇ J 5
```

A legitimate time not to ask for a suit in which you hold the ace (with suit preference or a discard) is when you suspect its layout looks like this. Your side will score two tricks if you wait for declarer to play it.

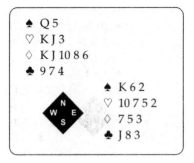

After 1NT(15-17) – 3NT, West leads the ♠J, covered all around. When declarer plays on diamonds, you play upwards. West takes the ace on the second round and continues with the ♠9.

What can you do on this spade? The rule here, with worthless cards, is to follow with the card that you would have returned. So you play the ♠6. If, instead, you started with K-6-3-2, you would play the ♠2. This way West, with an original holding of J-10-9-7, knows whether South's ♠8 will drop on the third round or whether it may be better to play safe.

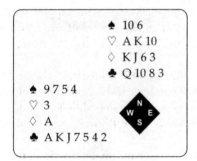

South, who has opened 1♡, plays in 4♡ after you have overcalled in clubs. You lead the ◊A and switch to the ♣K (king from ace-king after the first trick). When all follow, how do you continue?

If South has an opening bid, East can have only one high card, which means you will need to score both that and a diamond ruff. This only seems possible if that high card is the ♡Q. In this case, you need partner to ruff the second round of clubs with the ♡Q and play back a diamond. Of course, if you continue with the ♣A, East will not dream of ruffing. The right thing to do is to lead the ♣2. Your very low club is suit preference for a diamond back. Moreover, the fact you have underled the ♣A should warn partner that South might overruff a lower trump.

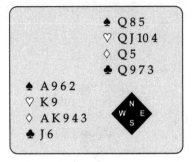

South opens a weak 1NT (12-14) and your double ends the bidding. With a sure entry, you lead the ◊A rather than the four and are pleased with this choice when dummy appears. You note partner's encouraging ◊8 and continue with the king to drop the queen while East plays the six.

You hope East started with J-8-6 and you want a heart back next so as to set up a heart to go with your five diamonds and a spade. The ◊3 would ask for a club and the ◊9 would ask for spade because this is a suit-preference situation. To ask for a heart you thus lead the ◊4.

Test Yourself

10.1

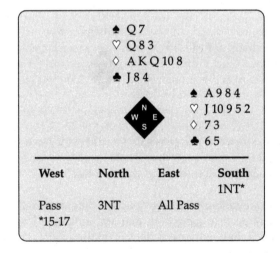

West	North	East	South
			1NT*
Pass	3NT	All Pass	
*15-17			

Partner leads the ♠3 and your ace drops declarer's ten. What card do you return?

10.2

```
              ♠ Q J
              ♡ J 5 4
              ◇ K 4 2
              ♣ K 10 9 8 2
                          ♠ 7 4
                    N     ♡ A Q 10 9 7 6 3
                 W     E  ◇ A 10
                    S     ♣ J 4
```

West	North	East	South
			1♠
Pass	1NT	2♡	3♠
Pass	4♠	All Pass	

Partner leads the ♡2 and your ace wins when South follows low. What do you return?

10.3

```
              ♠ Q J 7 3
              ♡ J 9
              ◇ A K J 8 5
              ♣ K 8
                          ♠ A 10 8 6
                    N     ♡ A 8 2
                 W     E  ◇ Q 10 4
                    S     ♣ 7 5 3
```

West	North	East	South
			1♣
Pass	1◇	Pass	1♠
Pass	4♠	All Pass	

Perhaps North should have bid 2♡ rather than jumping to 4♠. This is not your concern. Partner leads the ♡4 and your ace wins. What do you return? If you will excuse a question that is not really about signals, you might also think about what you plan to do later.

Solutions

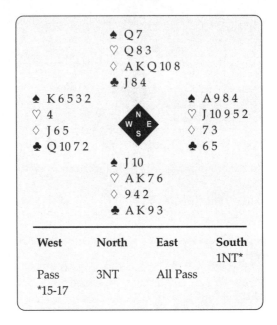

♠	Q 7		
♡	Q 8 3		
◇	A K Q 10 8		
♣	J 8 4		

♠ K 6 5 3 2   ♠ A 9 8 4
♡ 4   ♡ J 10 9 5 2
◇ J 6 5   ◇ 7 3
♣ Q 10 7 2   ♣ 6 5

♠ J 10
♡ A K 7 6
◇ 9 4 2
♣ A K 9 3

West	North	East	South
			1NT*
Pass	3NT	All Pass	
*15-17			

Partner leads the ♠3 and your ace drops declarer's ten. What card do you return?

With a minimum of 29 points between the opposing hands, prospects may not seem overly bright. Surely, you stand a chance only if the lead has caught declarer with a doubleton spade in each hand. Luckily, the fall of the ♠10 suggests that this is the case.

Actually, if you think about it, you probably need West to hold the ♠K. Declarer, with this card, is likely, one way or another, to have nine top tricks. For example, if West has the ♠J, ♡K and ♣Q, declarer will be able to make one spade, one heart, five diamonds and two clubs.

If the lead comes from K-J-x-x-x, your normal return of the ♠4 will do the trick. Partner will win with the king and, working out that you have returned your original fourth best, lead a low spade next. Unfortunately, if the ♠10 is a true card from J-10 doubleton, returning a low spade will block the suit. It is better to try the ♠9 instead. If the lead is from K-J-x-x-x, you will then unblock the ♠8 under the ♠J. On the actual layout, which is probably more likely, you will just have to hope that partner works out there is no hope unless the spades are running, and so wins the second round of spades to play a third.

10.2

```
                    ♠ Q J
                    ♡ J 5 4
                    ◇ K 4 2
                    ♣ K 10 9 8 2
  ♠ 9 8                            ♠ 7 4
  ♡ 2                              ♡ A Q 10 9 7 6 3
  ◇ Q 9 7 6 5 3         N          ◇ A 10
  ♣ Q 6 5 3          W   E         ♣ J 4
                        S
                    ♠ A K 10 6 5 3 2
                    ♡ K 8
                    ◇ J 8
                    ♣ A 7
```

West	North	East	South
			1♠
Pass	1NT	2♡	3♠
Pass	4♠	All Pass	

Partner leads the ♡2 and your ace wins. What do you return?

It looks right to return a heart for partner to ruff and the question is how high a heart to lead. You do not want a club back, so rule out the ♡3. With the ◇A as an entry it is tempting to return the ♡10, the highest card you can afford. The snag is that leading a third round of hearts is unlikely to promote a trump trick for partner. Therefore, unless partner can lead the ◇Q (from Q-J) you will end up with only three tricks: two aces and a ruff.

Given that you have no strong desire to regain the lead, you should make a more neutral return than the ♡10. The ♡7 feels about right. This will suggest values either in neither minor (in which case partner knows you are not going to defeat the contract) or, more likely, a little something in each. This being the case, partner will still lead the ◇Q if holding the ◇J as well but not lead from an unsupported queen. As the cards lie, a passive trump exit after ruffing the second round of hearts puts the contract one down.

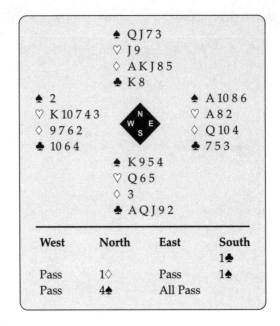

West	North	East	South
			1♣
Pass	1◊	Pass	1♠
Pass	4♠	All Pass	

Perhaps North should have bid 2♡ rather than jumping to 4♠. This is not your concern. Partner leads the ♡4 and your ace wins. What do you return? If you will excuse a question that is not really about signals, you might also think about what you plan to do later.

There are two genuine chances to defeat the contract. The first is that West has the ♡K and a singleton ♣9. In this case, after a heart return, you will score two hearts and two trumps. The second chance is that West has a singleton ♠K, in which case you make three trump tricks.

Your best hope, however, is that West has the ♡K and that declarer takes a losing view in trumps. With a holding of K-9-x-x facing Q-J-x-x the natural play is small to the jack and, whether it wins or loses, to play the queen next. This will set up a marked finesse if, as is the case, you have four trumps including the ten.

To throw declarer off the scent you plan to play the ♠8 on the first round. This will create the losing option of playing West for A-10-x-x and be safe for you if West has the singleton ♣9.

As a preparatory move, you should try to make it look like you have four hearts rather than three. This will make it a little bit more plausible that you have a singleton trump. You do this by returning the ♡2.

More on Continuations and Returns in Brief

- You do not return your original fourth highest if you need to hold the lead or if doing so will block the suit.

- When you have most of the defensive strength, you can make a non-standard return to try to deceive declarer.

- Returning your fifth highest will tend to make your holding look weaker than it is, while returning your third highest will have the opposite effect.

- If you can give partner only one ruff, it may not be right to give a suit-preference signal for a suit in which you have a quick entry.

- If partner leads the same suit as originally, you normally follow with the card that you would have returned.

- If you have the top card in a suit but want partner to ruff the next round of it, underlead your high card.

- If it is possible that you will want any of three suits back when you are clearing your suit in a no-trump contract, a middle card asks for the middle suit.

Chapter 11
More on Leading New Suits

For declarer, some plays are difficult to execute with confidence, a backward finesse for example. Defenders stand a better chance.

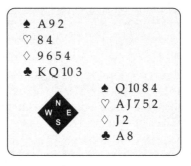

You open 1♡, South overcalls 2◊, West raises to 2♡ and North's 3◊ ends the auction. West leads the ♡3 and your ace wins.

To defeat the contract you will probably need two spade tricks to go with two hearts (you hope) and a club. With the threat that declarer can take discards on the clubs, you must attack spades yourself. If West holds K-J-x, a 'normal' ♠4 will work fine. Alas, it will not be so good if South has J-x-x. Partner will have to put up the ♠K and you will only get one spade trick. The right card to lead is the ♠10, just as if you had the ♠9 that is actually in dummy. After the ♠10 is covered all around, you will aim to put partner in with the ♡K to lead a second spade.

A first cousin to the spade suit above is the club suit shown here. If, as East, you switch to the ♣5, South ducks and West has to play the ace. The right card is the ♣J and then you can make three tricks (four in a no-trump contract) whatever South does. If North were declarer, so that you could see Q-x-x in dummy, again it would be right to lead the jack.

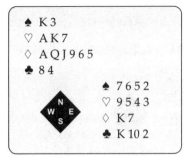

North opens 1◇ and raises South's 1NT to game. West leads the ♠Q. Declarer takes the ♠A and runs the ◇10 to your king. What do you do next?

It is clear to everyone that declarer has at least nine tricks ready to run: five diamonds and ace-king in each major. You therefore need to take the next four tricks. If West holds ♣A-Q-J-x or A-J-9-x, it does not matter which club you lead, but can you cater for other holdings? If you lead the ♣10, you save the ♣K as a re-entry as well as unblocking the suit. Now you only need West to hold A-J-7-x or A-Q-7-x:

After the ten goes to the queen and ace, partner puts you back in with the king. A further club lead will pick up South's remaining holding.

Leading low from Q-x-x is not always right. Suppose you are East here and know that your side needs three fast diamond tricks. In this case, you need to lead the queen, not a low card. If you led low, South would duck and West would be on lead. The position would be equivalent if you had J-x-x. To score three fast tricks you would need partner to hold A-Q-10-x. Again you would need to lead high to take advantage of this.

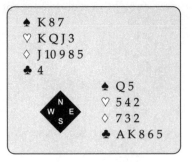

After North-South bid 1♡ – 4♡, West leads the ♣10 to your king.

With one club trick and probably no trump tricks available, you figure to need two diamonds and a spade (or the other way round). If you lead the ♠Q and find partner with the J-10-x-x-(x) of spades and two winners in diamonds, you will beat the contract. A switch to the ♠Q works less well if West's spades are only ♠J-9-x-x-(x). Most likely, declarer wins the first spade in dummy and partner cannot continue the suit safely. You do better to lead the ♠5 instead.

Before moving on, I will mention that it is routine to lead low from a doubleton in trumps. You want to keep whatever strength you have.

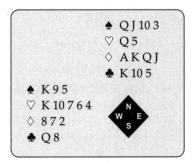

North opens 1◊ and raises South's 1♠ to 3♠ to end the bidding. You lead the ♡6 to partner's ace. When the ♡3 comes back, South plays the jack and your king wins.

With two hearts in the bag and a trump trick to come, you presumably need either two club tricks, or one club and a ruff. Do you see the snag in leading the ♣Q? East, with A-x-x-x-x, will capture dummy's king and play one back, expecting you to hold the ♣J. A better bet is to try the ♣8, which partner is more likely to duck. Then you can get your ruff.

Easy Guide to Defensive Signals at Bridge

In a similar vein, it may be right to fool declarer into thinking that you have a sequence when you do not or *vice versa*.

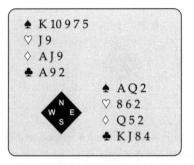

South opens 1♡ (five-card majors), North bids 1♠, South rebids 1NT and North bids 3NT. West leads the ◊3 and your ◊Q wins the trick.

Apart from the ◊K, West must have a Yarborough, making prospects bleak. With your two entries, you might set up and cash two club tricks, but how can this help? Declarer will come to nine tricks by way of five hearts, two clubs (the ♣A and ♣Q) and two diamonds (via a finesse).

What you need to do is to hope that West has ♣10-x-x and convince declarer that the club suit is like this. On this layout, it would be right not to cover the ♣J with the ♣Q and, if you led the suit again, to play low from hand again. So, with your actual hand, switch to the ♣J!

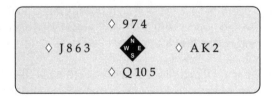

Suppose you are East and your side needs three quick diamond tricks. In this case, you must lead the ◊2. Since it caters for a lead from K-J-2 or A-J-2, declarer is likely to duck, but now West's ◊J will win a trick.

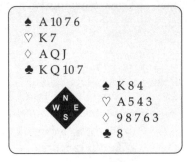

North opens 1♣ and raises South's 1♠ response to game. West leads the
♡J and you capture dummy's king with the ace.

You surely need to find partner with the ♣A and score a ruff to beat the
contract. The problem is that if you return the ♣8, it will look like the top
of a doubleton and West will duck. If your trump winner were the ace,
you could stop this from happening by cashing the ♠A, which would
preclude playing you for a doubleton. On your actual hand, the best
switch is to the ◊9. Then, when you come in with the ♠K and lead the ♣8,
there is a great chance partner will be able to work out you cannot be out
of diamonds (or hold the ◊K) and do the right thing.

After the opponents bid 1♡ – 3♡ – 4♡, West leads the ◊3 to the queen and
ace. The lead would appear to be from K-x-x-x-(x), in which case you can
score a diamond ruff to beat the contract.

Although there is no danger here that West will duck the ◊K, you need
to watch out for something else. Given that you would return the ◊10
from A-10-x, it may appear more attractive to lead a spade through the
king than to try to give you a ruff. The solution is to exclude that option
by cashing the ♠A before returning the ◊10. It will surely be clear that the
♠A is not a singleton and you will get your ruff this way.

Test Yourself

11.1

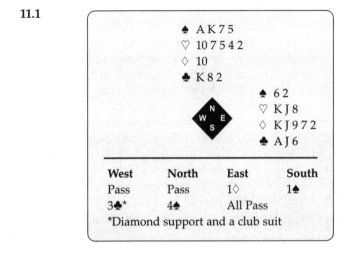

	♠ A K 7 5		
	♡ 10 7 5 4 2		
	◇ 10		
	♣ K 8 2		

West	North	East	South
Pass	Pass	1◇	1♠
3♣*	4♠	All Pass	

*Diamond support and a club suit

East hand: ♠ 6 2 ♡ K J 8 ◇ K J 9 7 2 ♣ A J 6

Partner leads the ◇6 and your king loses to the ace. Declarer draws trumps in two rounds, West throwing the ◇5 on the second. Next comes the ♣10 to the seven, king and ace. Which card do you return?

11.2

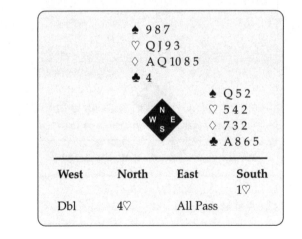

	♠ 9 8 7		
	♡ Q J 9 3		
	◇ A Q 10 8 5		
	♣ 4		

East hand: ♠ Q 5 2 ♡ 5 4 2 ◇ 7 3 2 ♣ A 8 6 5

West	North	East	South
			1♡
Dbl	4♡	All Pass	

Partner leads the ♣Q and your ace wins. What do you return?

11.3

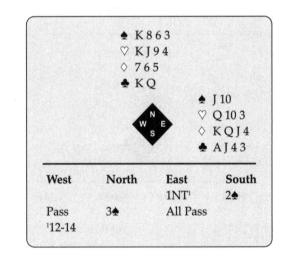

	♠ Q J 10 8	
	♡ A 6	
	◊ Q 9 6 5	
	♣ Q 9 3	
		♠ K 9
		♡ Q J 3
		◊ 7 3 2
		♣ K J 10 5 4

West	North	East	South
		Pass	1NT[1]
Pass	2♣	Dbl	2◊[2]
Pass	3NT	All Pass	

[1]15-17

[2]Four (+) diamonds and no four-card major

Heeding your double, partner leads the ♣8. Dummy plays the nine and your ten wins. What do you return?

11.4

	♠ K 8 6 3	
	♡ K J 9 4	
	◊ 7 6 5	
	♣ K Q	
		♠ J 10
		♡ Q 10 3
		◊ K Q J 4
		♣ A J 4 3

West	North	East	South
		1NT[1]	2♠
Pass	3♠	All Pass	

[1]12-14

Partner leads the ♣10 and you win with the ace. Which cunning return can you find?

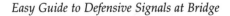

11.1

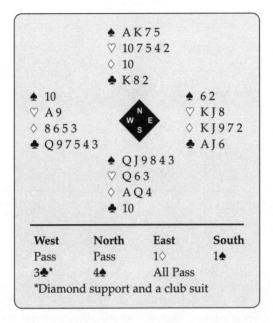

West	North	East	South
Pass	Pass	1◊	1♠
3♣*	4♠	All Pass	

*Diamond support and a club suit

Partner leads the ◊6 and your king loses to the ace. Declarer draws trumps in two rounds, West throwing the ◊5 on the second. Next comes the ♣10 to the seven, king and ace. Which card do you return?

Since the ◊6 cannot have been fourth highest, you can place South with the ◊Q. West's ♣7 is also revealing. As a high card it must be showing an even number of clubs, six no doubt on the bidding. If you can score only one trick in the minors and none in trumps, you will need three heart tricks. How can you get them?

If South has a doubleton heart (unlikely) or the ♡A or Q-9-x, you are going to be out of luck. You need West to hold A-9 doubleton. To take advantage of this you need to make the 'surrounding' play or backward finesse I mentioned at the start of the chapter. You lead the ♡J. If South ducks this or covers now but ducks partner's return of the nine, you cannot score all three heart tricks at once. This does not matter. You will score the ♡K later.

If you fail to return a heart, declarer can arrange to ruff one club in hand, discard the other on the ◊Q and ruff a diamond in dummy. Then, if declarer correctly ducks the first round of hearts, partner will have to win the second round and concede a ruff-and-discard.

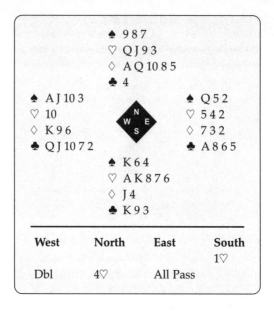

West	North	East	South
			1♡
Dbl	4♡	All Pass	

Partner leads the ♣Q and your ace wins. What do you return?

With any diamond finesses working for the other side, the defenders can score only one trick in the minors. If West happens to have a trump winner, two spade tricks will suffice. More likely, you will need three.

Given that declarer, upon gaining the lead, will be able to cash the ♣K and discard a spade from dummy, the three spade tricks need to come at once. You must hope West has A-J-10-(x) and switch to the ♠Q.

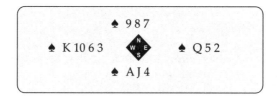

Lest you think that it is generally a good idea to lead high from Q-x-x, consider this more common layout. If you lead the ♠Q and it loses to the ace, your side can only score two tricks easily if you, rather than partner, gain the lead. It is better, when you do not need three fast tricks, to lead low. This caters to the layout shown, and for when South has K-J-x and two slow spade tricks will suffice. Leading low also works better if declarer has K-J-(x) and you need two fast spade tricks because it leaves the chance of a wrong guess.

```
                    ♠ Q J 10 8
                    ♡ A 6
                    ◇ Q 9 6 5
                    ♣ Q 9 3
    ♠ 7 5 3 2                        ♠ K 9
    ♡ 9 7 5 4 2         N            ♡ Q J 3
    ◇ A 4          W        E        ◇ 7 3 2
    ♣ 8 6              S             ♣ K J 10 5 4
                    ♠ A 6 4
                    ♡ K 10 8
                    ◇ K J 10 8
                    ♣ A 7 2
```

West	North	East	South
		Pass	1NT[1]
Pass	2♣	Dbl	2◇[2]
Pass	3NT	All Pass	

[1]15-17

[2]Four (+) diamonds and no four-card major

Heeding your double, partner leads the ♣8. Dummy plays the nine and your ten wins. What do you return?

The lead looks like top of a doubleton, which means that playing a club back will give a trick to dummy's queen. It might seem that the natural switch is to a diamond. A closer inspection reveals otherwise. Suppose West has the ◇A or ◇K and wins this to continue clubs. How will you get in? South must have the rest of the high cards, including the ♠A.

For similar reasons, you can dismiss a heart switch. If the ♡K is on your left, you will not be able to set up anything, while if West has that card, declarer will have the rest of the high cards .

You need to lead a spade and, for two reasons, it needs to be the nine. The first is that West may have the ♠A; in this case, you want a club through the queen before your ♠K entry has gone. The second is that a low spade may give declarer a nasty guess; on the actual layout, letting the spade run makes the contract. However, if you had the ◇A and West the ♠K, it would be better to rise with the ♠A and knock out your ◇A. If you make a habit of giving your opponents guesses to make, they are bound to get some of them wrong.

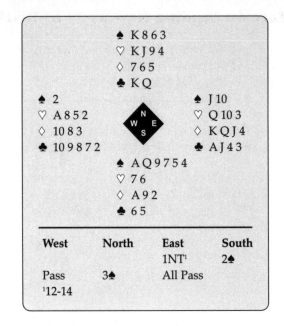

	♠ K 8 6 3	
	♡ K J 9 4	
	◇ 7 6 5	
	♣ K Q	

♠ 2		♠ J 10
♡ A 8 5 2	N	♡ Q 10 3
◇ 10 8 3	W E	◇ K Q J 4
♣ 10 9 8 7 2	S	♣ A J 4 3

	♠ A Q 9 7 5 4	
	♡ 7 6	
	◇ A 9 2	
	♣ 6 5	

West	North	East	South
		1NT¹	2♠
Pass	3♠	All Pass	
¹12-14			

Partner leads the ♣10 and you win with the ace. Which cunning return can you find?

There are three aces missing and it seems clear that South has two out of the three. (If West had none, you would be defending 4♠). North's simple raise was quite cautious and you will probably need South to have three diamonds to give you a chance. Which ace will be of most use in partner's hand?

The ♠A, which is unlikely in any event, can hardly help. Assuming that South has six spades, you will make at most four tricks. Two diamonds to go with the black aces is your maximum entitlement.

The ◇A, unless it is accompanied by an improbable ♠Q, will not help much either. That will give you at best three diamonds and a club.

The ♡A is the most helpful card West can hold. Now, if South is 2-3 in the red suits and misguesses the heart layout, you might score two tricks in each red suit to go with the ♣A. Unfortunately, your 1NT opening defines your strength within a narrow range and declarer may be able to work out that you would be out of range if you held the ♡A. Can you see a way to lead your opponent astray? Instead of an honest ◇K, try leading the ◇Q! Placing West with the ◇K, declarer may well put you with the ♡A and go one down.

More on Leading New Suits in Brief

- When you have almost an interior sequence and can see the missing card from the sequence on your right (or can see the card you wish to capture on your left), lead as if you had that missing card. This may allow you to take a backward finesse.

- If you need three tricks quickly and the opponent on your right has low cards, it can be right to lead high from Q-x-x or J-x-x.

- With a three-card holding including two high cards, you may need to start with the middle card to avoid blocking the suit.

- In the trump suit, you normally lead low from a doubleton or four cards and middle from three regardless of your strength.

- You may need to lead low from a useful doubleton in a plain suit if partner has your side's only possible entries.

- It may also be necessary to lead low from a useful doubleton to make sure that partner does not think you have a sequence.

- If you can see that normal defensive strategy will fail, you can attempt to deceive declarer by pretending to hold a sequence when you do not or by underleading a sequence.

- If your intentions may not be clear to partner, look for a way to clarify them, if necessary switching suits or cashing an ace so that partner knows not to try a losing alternative.

Chapter 12
Non-standard methods

Some people play that on partner's lead you always signal *attitude* or you always signal *count*. Although this is less efficient than my suggested methods, playing that a signal has the same meaning whatever dummy's holding does reduce the risk of misunderstandings. If you are new to using signals, you might choose to start with using only one type or the other. Then, after a month or so of practice, you could use the other type before moving on to the methods I suggest.

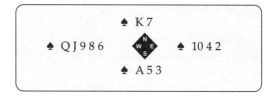

This example is on page 10 and you will see that count signals do not work well. If West leads the queen and East plays the two under the king to show an odd number, South could have either A-10-x or A-x-x.

This is the heart suit from the top of page 14 and this time attitude signals do not work. Suppose you are West and East discourages with the three under your king. You will not know whether your queen will stand up on the next round or whether, as on this layout, attempting to cash the queen will merely set up dummy's jack for a possible discard.

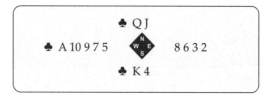

This is the club suit from the bottom of page 14. Again an attitude ♣2 from East will be of no use whatsoever in helping West to work out whether South has K-x (as shown) or K-x-x.

Of course, there are layouts for which either method proves effective. If you are West and defending a suit contract, you will often want to know whether South has three spades or two. Now East would play the ten from 10-2 either to encourage or to show an even number and the two from 10-6-2 either to discourage or to show an odd number.

In my experience, and that of most European experts, it is better, if you must choose between count and attitude, to play count. The reason is that it is easier to work out where the high cards are from the play to a trick than it is to tell how many cards each player has in the suit.

Some players combine using attitude and count signals but with rigid divisions between the two. One popular method with an alliterative name is *ace for attitude, king for count*. What this means is that on the lead of the ace you encourage or discourage, mainly based on whether you hold the queen. On the lead of the king, you give a count signal.

You need to choose your lead from the ace-king carefully. Lead the ace if there is a chance you can score three tricks in the suit if partner has the queen. Lead the king if your length means you want to know whether your side has one trick or two. In a suit that your side has not bid and supported, lead the ace from a three- or four-card holding. With five or more cards, if your side has found a fit in the suit, or you hold the queen, lead the king. Also lead the king against a slam contract regardless of your length as you just need two rounds to stand up. Some play that you also do this against a contract at the five level.

With the last holding, West leads the ace to find out whether East has the queen (or, in a trump contract, a doubleton). When East encourages with the eight, it is safe to continue. Swap the East and South holdings and East, now with 10-6-5, would discourage, suggesting that West switches.

With greater length, there is no chance of three tricks against a suit contract if East has Q-x-x. Accordingly, West leads the king to find out how many diamonds everyone has. When East shows an odd number and the queen falls, West knows the danger of continuing the suit.

The downside with *ace for attitude, king for count* tends to come when you have a king-queen combination and really want to know who has the jack rather than whether partner has an odd or even number.

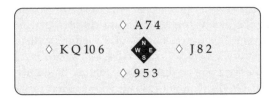

If you lead the ◊K and it goes to the four, two and three, you have a guess as to who has J-x-x and who has x-x-x. Some seek to get around this by playing that you signal attitude on the lead of the ace or queen and that you lead the queen from a weak king-queen holding. The snag with this is that the player in third seat may, when holding the ace, needlessly overtake for fear declarer has a singleton king. On the layout below, wasting the ace on the queen sets up dummy's ten on the third round. In summary, *ace for attitude, king for count* seems an improvement on *attitude always* or *count always* but not on the main methods given in this book.

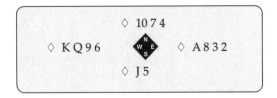

Some pairs play certain leads as a *request to unblock*. Historically, the lead of the ace against a no-trump contract asked the leader's partner to unblock any honour held. The thinking was that against a no-trump contract you would often lead low from an ace-king holding, which meant you were giving up little to play this. In practice, if you have a side entry or your suit is only A-K-x-x or A-K-x, you might want to lead high. This means that the risk of confusing partner as to whether you hold king-queen or ace-king is higher than originally thought. Partly for this reason the method has fallen into disuse.

If you do play the ace as a *request to unblock*, you need a suit as good as A-K-J-10-(x) or A-K-Q-10-(x) to use it. As the leader's partner, you unblock if you can or, if you have no picture cards, signal count.

Perhaps more popular now is to play that leading the second-highest card from a sequence serves as a *request to unblock*. On this method, you lead the king from A-K-J-10-x and the queen from K-Q-10-9-x. In third seat, you will either have a collection of low cards or, if you do not, it will be obvious what has happened. If the lead is the king and you hold the queen, partner cannot have led from an average king-queen holding and so must have led from A-K-J-10-x or similar. Likewise if you hold the jack when partner leads the queen, you can work out that the lead comes from K-Q-10-9-x or similar. Players using this method tend to play *count always*. There is little point in discouraging with a low card when your failure to unblock is telling partner that anyway.

You cannot play a *request to unblock* and *ace for attitude* at the same time because you need the play of the queen under the king to show queen-jack when the king is led in the *ace for attitude* style. What you could do is to play the *request to unblock* only against no-trump contracts and *ace for attitude* only against suit contracts.

A final variation on the unblocking theme is to play *strong king* leads. This means you only lead the king if you want an unblock. It resembles the old-fashioned ace lead, except now you might have K-Q-10-9-x or A-K-J-10-x. With an ace-king combination too weak to invite partner to unblock you have no problem. You lead the ace. The problem comes, just as we saw on the previous page, when you have king-queen but not enough strength to have partner unblock. Then you have to lead the queen, which causes as many problems as the method seeks to solve. By the simple expedient of playing attitude signals in the right way you avoid the need for special unblocking cards, and therefore I would not particularly recommend any of the methods on this page.

Reverse count and *reverse attitude* are by far the most worthwhile of the non-standard methods you will find in this chapter. With *reverse count*, a low card shows an even number in the suit while a high spot card shows an odd number in the suit. With *reverse attitude,* a low card encourages and a high card discourages. You can reverse the attitude but not the count, but for simplicity I shall I assume they go together.

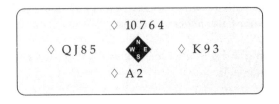

If West leads the ◊Q, East can encourage, using reverse signals, by playing the three. This is clearly better than having to play the nine to encourage, which standard attitude signals would entail doing.

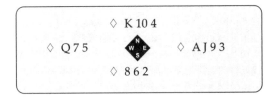

On standard methods, if East wants to discard a diamond and ask West to lead the suit, it is necessary to waste the nine. Reverse signals allow East to ask for the suit by discarding the three. If, as East, you had a worthless holding, say 9-6-3-2, you could easily spare the six and maybe the nine. This means you lose little by playing reverse signals. Actually reverse signals produce their biggest gain when you have a doubleton. You may like to revisit page 25 and you will see there that West had to play low from ◊9-3 to avoid conceding a trick. With 10-x or J-x, it is still more likely that you must save your higher card.

What are the disadvantages? Reverse signals can be less clear. For example, using standard count, your lowest card from three will often be so low that partner can instantly place you with three. Using reverse count, people tend to play middle from three and this may be harder to read. The other thing is that, when giving count, you play your lowest card from a doubleton or four, making it harder for partner to tell these holdings apart. Despite this, reverse signals seem to offer a technical advantage. When you add this to the fact that they currently have surprise value (with so few people playing them), they are well worth considering.

Easy Guide to Defensive Signals at Bridge

The *obvious shift* signal is a modified attitude signal. With *obvious shift* you encourage partner's lead either if you like the suit or if you cannot stand a switch to the most obvious other suit. What constitutes the *obvious shift* suit depends a bit on the bidding and on the cards in dummy. If declarer has bid one or no suits, then dummy's weakest suit (assuming declarer has not bid it) is the *obvious shift* suit. Weakest in this context normally equates to shortest. If, however, declarer has a side suit, you may decide that this is not the *obvious shift* suit and that dummy's side suit is the *obvious shift* suit. On the first example on page 11, you will see that East does not want a switch to either spades or clubs. So, no matter which suit the *obvious shift* suit is, it would be right to encourage, just as I recommended using standard methods.

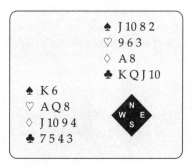

This deal shows *obvious shift* working well. After the opponents have bid 1♠ – 3♠ – 4♠, you lead the ◊J to the ace, two and five. Declarer runs the ♠J to the king and you must decide what to do.

If partner's ◊2 said: 'I do not have the ◊K' (attitude), or: 'I have an odd number of diamonds' (count), you face an awkward guess. The right move depends upon who has the ♡K and who has the ♣A. Playing *obvious shift* you do not have a problem. East would only discourage diamonds if able to stand a heart switch, making it safe to cash the ♡A (or, if you had A-J-x, to lead a low heart).

Despite the occasional goal on a layout like this, *obvious shift* signals strike me as inferior. Surely, on most hands you are more interested in knowing whether partner likes the suit you have led than one you have not. If you do not want to know that, you are more likely to want to get a count signal than to know about some other suit. There is also the possibility of a misunderstanding about which suit is the *obvious shift*. Indeed, the fact that the *obvious shift* signal enjoys virtually no support outside North America speaks for itself.

The *Smith peter* differs from giving a count or suit-preference signal on any suit led by an opponent. On the first suit declarer leads, a high or low card indicates only whether or not you like the suit led at trick one.

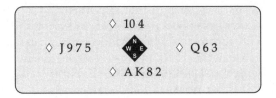

Suppose on the first trick West leads the ◇5, East puts up the queen and the ace wins. Both defenders will then want to know who has the ◇K. Whatever other suit declarer plays, the defenders will play low if they can, each saying they are not very interested in diamonds. If one or other of them had the ◇K, that player would start a high-low.

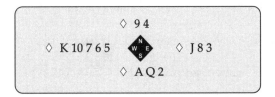

The *Smith peter* really comes into its own in unearthing a false card. Let us say that West leads the ◇6 and declarer, terrified of a switch to some other suit, wins the ◇J with the ace. If you are West, you will no doubt place East with the ◇Q and continue the suit when you regain the lead. If, however, you play *Smith peters*, East's failure to give or begin a high-low signal on the suit declarer plays tells you otherwise.

Some people reverse the *Smith peter* for the opening leader. In other words, starting a high-low says: 'Please do not return my suit.' The thinking behind this is that it is normal to return partner's suit, which means a signal should ask for something unusual.

Smith peters fit best with *always count* signals and perhaps with third and fifth leads, when the defenders cannot tell each other's strength in the suit first led. Conversely, if you play *always attitude* signals or play attitude leads, the times when a *Smith peter* will prove helpful will be far fewer. Although some people swear by *Smith peters*, I have never found them very useful. On the vast majority of deals, there is some other way to impart the information that a *Smith peter* would convey, and I do not like to give up all the normal signals on an opposing lead.

Suit-preference discards or, as you may hear them called, *McKenney* or *Lavinthal discards*, are by far the most popular variation on standard methods covered in this chapter. Indeed, amongst tournament players they are probably more popular than natural discards.

```
♠ A 10 7
♡ 7
◇ 9 7 5 4 2
♣ K Q 10 7
```

Suppose you hold this hand and declarer leads two rounds of hearts. On the second round, you are likely to want to discard a diamond and to signal for clubs as you do so. To achieve this you let go your lowest diamond, the two. A low card asks for the lower of the two suits excluding the one led and the one discarded. If you wanted to ask for a spade instead, you would discard the highest diamond you could afford, probably the nine. To express neutral preference between the two other suits, you discard a middling card, in this case the five.

The discard of a middling card is also a backdoor way, though not a strong one, of asking for the suit you discard. (Having no preference between the other two suits could mean you have values in both, in which case you may have nothing in the suit discarded. Alternatively, it could mean that you possess little in either of those suits and hence perhaps something in the suit you discard.)

Without doubt, *suit-preference discards* prove effective when you have a suit that you want partner to lead and can afford to let go a card in some other suit. They do not work so well if you can only spare cards in one suit and want partner to know you have that suit well held or if you need to give a count or some other special signal. You also need to watch the spot cards carefully and picture which are missing so that you do not confuse a neutral card with a more definite signal.

The simplicity of the method, combined with the fact that all players who use signals employ suit-preference signals in other situations, may explain its popularity. Revisiting Chapter 3, *suit-preference* discards would work just about acceptably on all the examples and quiz deals. For example on page 40, West would discard the ♣J on hand (i) and the ♠5 on hand (ii). In Chapter 8, they would not work quite so well. For instance, they would be useless on the deal on page 115.

Count discards are another simple method. You throw suits you do not want and show your length as you do so. A discard of, say, the ♣9, says: 'I have an even number of clubs and no great interest in the suit.' Likewise a discard of the ♣3 says: 'I have an odd number of clubs and no great interest in the suit'. The strength of the method is that you throw losers – invariably a good idea. A drawback, it would seem, is that you cannot request a suit unless you can afford to throw the top of a sequence. In practice, you can often get round this. On many deals, there will be only two suits you might want. In this case, you discard the one that you do not want. If there are three suits and you can make two discards, you discard one card from each of the two unwanted suits.

Looking at Chapter 3 again, on all but one deal *Count discards* would work reasonably. The problem is on page 39:

> ♠ J 8
> ♡ Q 8 7 6 3 2
> ◇ A K 9 8
> ♣ 2

This was your hand as East and you want to discard on the second round of clubs, asking for a diamond as you do so. You would have to discard a heart, this time the eight, which would tend to put partner off hearts but would do nothing to suggest diamonds. A *suit-preference* discard of the ♡3, by contrast, would be crystal clear.

> ♠ 10 5 4
> ♡ 9 8 6 4 2
> ◇ 4
> ♣ Q 7 4 3

This was the one slightly awkward hand for *suit-preference discards* in Chapter 3. Partner held this hand and wanted to deny interest in hearts when you led two rounds of diamonds. To convey this message clearly East would, using that method, need to discard the ♣7. Playing *count discards* the more natural discard of the ♡2 does the job. In Chapter 9, obviously *count discards* work better than *suit preference* on page 115 but it is the other way round on page 120. *Count discards* also make it easier to conceal your holding on page 122. Overall, both methods are playable and only fractionally inferior to 'standard' methods.

Odd-even discards seek to get around the slight weaknesses in the two previous methods. The discard of an odd card, no matter how high or low it is, encourages the suit discarded. The discard of an even card discourages the suit and expresses suit preference between the other two. So, with ◊A-10-8-5-3-2 and spades led, you discard the ◊3 to ask for a diamond, the ◊2 to ask for a club and the ◊8 or, if you can afford it, the ◊10, to ask for spades.

The strength of the method is that you can, assuming you have the right cards, discard from whichever suit you want. The problem is that often you will not have exactly the right cards. For example, if you have only one even card, you cannot give an effective suit-preference signal. The other trouble is that you may have only odd cards but not want the suit. If you can make two discards from the suit, you get round this by playing high-low with odd cards, which cancels the original message.

(i)	(ii)
♠ A Q J 9 5	♠ Q J 9 8 5
♡ J 8 3	♡ J 8 3
◊ 4	◊ 4
♣ J 10 6 5	♣ A J 10 5

If we go back to the hand on page 40 again, West discards the ♣10 (clearer than the ♡8) on hand (i) but has no very effective discard with hand (ii). With no low even cards in either spades or hearts, the ♠8 is the best West can do.

Odd-even discards present no problem for East on the hand on page 48 and repeated on the previous page. The ♡8, ostensibly asking for a spade, will deny the ♡K without actively asking for a club.

Some people find the method easier to remember by playing the even cards as encouraging and the odd cards as discouraging or, if you like another alliterative description coined by Ron Klinger, 'off-putting'.

A further variation, particularly with the alternative method, is to play odd cards as asking for the other suit of the same colour rather than as suit preference. This is because you normally have only four usable odd cards, the nine, seven, five and three, which reduces your options to signal suit preference. Playing this variation, called by some *Dodd discards*, an odd diamond would ask for a heart and an even one for a diamond, with the lower the card the stronger the message.

Revolving discards are a close relation to *suit-preference discards*. The key difference is that you consider the four suits as a continuum or as points on a circle, say with clubs at 12 o'clock, diamonds at 3 o'clock, hearts at 6 o'clock and spades at 9 o'clock. This generally gives you two ways to ask for a suit. A high card asks for the next suit clockwise while a low card asks for the next suit anticlockwise. A middle card, if you have one, is neutral, asking for neither.

(i)	(ii)
♠ A 9 5 3	♠ J 9 5 3
♡ 8 6 2	♡ K 8 2
◇ 7 5	◇ 7 5
♣ A 9 4 2	♣ A 9 4 2

These were the East hands on page 42 and, if you recall, declarer was running diamonds. You may also recall that East had played the ♣A and the ♣2 and wanted to tell West whether it was necessary to keep spades or hearts. With (i) East now has two ways to signal for spades, either with a high heart, the eight, or a low club, the four. Likewise with (ii) East may have two ways to signal strength in hearts. Clearest is to throw the ♠3, the low card asking for the suit immediately below spades. The ♣9, if not deemed a neutral card, should also do the trick.

Revolving discards have a technical advantage over *suit-preference discards* because you can ask for spades without having to use a high card to do so. They do, however, require greater mental agility, which may explain why they are less popular.

You need to discuss one important issue with your partner. Let us say a heart is led. What does a high diamond discard mean? Does it ask (notionally) for a heart, meaning it is actually neutral? Alternatively, do you exclude hearts from the circle, meaning it asks for the next around the circle, in this case spades?

There is one more issue, which applies both for *revolving discards* and *suit-preference discards*. If, in a suit contract, you discard on a plain suit, what does a signal for the trump suit mean? For example, if hearts are trumps and you discard a high diamond on a spade, do you really want partner to lead trumps? The alternative meaning is more neutral, mainly saying (since you chose not to discard a low diamond) that you do not want to ask for a club. The latter is the more common treatment. The most important thing is that you and your partner agree.

Although you might think I have given you many suit-preference signals in this book, some people play even more.

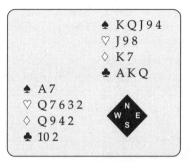

You may remember this layout from page 106. South is in 3NT and your lead of the ♡3 goes to the nine, ten and ace. When South then leads the ♠10, I suggested that you held up your ace on the second round to allow partner to give you a suit-preference signal.

You may have spotted that this involved a slight risk. South, if holding a six-card club suit, could have nine top tricks after you duck the first spade. You can avoid this risk if, as some experts do, you play that a suit-preference signal can apply on the first round of an opposing suit if it is clear that a count signal will be of little help. In this case, you can afford to take your ace on the first round. You would expect partner to play a high spade with the ♡K or a low one with good diamonds.

The reason why only a minority use a suit-preference signal on the first round of a suit is that one can rarely be sure that a count signal is no use.

Suppose this is a side suit and West decides to grab the ♣A when South leads the three. You could argue that, since West has already decided not to hold up, there is no point in a count signal from East. Well, if West knows that declarer has a singleton and so cannot reach dummy's clubs, it will probably be right to defend passively. If, instead, East (with a club fewer) were to signal a doubleton, it might be right, if trumps are still out, to return the suit or, if not, to try to cash out.

One other area in which some play more *suit-preference signals* is in the trump suit. The times are rare when you want to play high-low to indicate a third trump and a desire to ruff, or for the other reasons given in Chapter 8. If you are willing to give those up completely, you could make a suit-preference signal on the first round of trumps. Although I did not say so explicitly in Chapter 8, you can give a suit-preference signal on the second round (if you began with at least three trumps), with standard methods. If you play *trump suit preference signals*, they apply when you lead trumps as well. In this case, you do not routinely lead a low trump from a low doubleton. Consider this example:

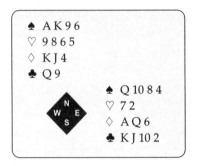

$$
\begin{array}{l}
\spadesuit\ A\,K\,9\,6 \\
\heartsuit\ 9\,8\,6\,5 \\
\diamondsuit\ K\,J\,4 \\
\clubsuit\ Q\,9
\end{array}
$$

$$
\begin{array}{l}
\spadesuit\ Q\,10\,8\,4 \\
\heartsuit\ 7\,2 \\
\diamondsuit\ A\,Q\,6 \\
\clubsuit\ K\,J\,10\,2
\end{array}
$$

After you open a 12-14 1NT, South, who does not have a conventional bid available, overcalls 2♡ and North raises to 4♡. West leads the ◇7 to the jack and queen.

It looks like West needs to have either the ♣A or a trump trick and, to allow for both possibilities, you might switch to a trump. What you hope is that West wins and switches to a club. Unfortunately, that might not be such a bright idea if your hand were this:

$$
\begin{array}{l}
\spadesuit\ Q\,J\,8\,4 \\
\heartsuit\ 7\,2 \\
\diamondsuit\ A\,Q\,10 \\
\clubsuit\ K\,10\,4\,2
\end{array}
$$

Assuming it is clear from the dummy that you cannot want a spade, you could use the ♡7, your higher heart, to ask for the higher minor with this alternative hand. With your actual hand, you will lead the ♡2 to ask for a club. Perhaps on this particular deal you might argue that your 1NT makes a ruff unlikely and so suit preference should apply anyway. Still, an agreement reduces the risk of misunderstanding.

You know that if you return a suit partner led originally, you return your higher remaining card if you started with a three-card suit and your original fourth best if you started with four. The effect is that you lead high when you have two cards left and low when you have three. In other words, you are giving a count signal as if you started with what you have left. This standard treatment is an example of the *remaining count* signal. You may also recall that on a couple of occasions I suggested that you followed with, or discarded, the card you would have returned. For example, on page 117 you played the ♡Q from Q-5-4 on the first trick and then plumped for the ♡5 as your discard. This again accorded with the *remaining count* signal. Some people go the whole hog and say that, unless you gave a count signal on the first round of a suit, you always show *remaining count*.

What does this mean you do differently? If you led fourth highest from a five-card suit, you have four cards left, which is an even number. This means you play upwards next time, not your original fifth highest. To play down you would need to have started with six cards or two. (You cannot play downwards from a remaining three-card holding if you led your lowest card from the original four). Likewise, if you started with five cards in partner's suit, you do not return your original fourth best. You will have an even number left and so need to return a higher card.

The other thing really to watch out for is if you discard from a suit that your side led. Suppose you start with Q-9-7-6-4-2 and lead the six on the first round. If you are playing natural or suit-preference discards, you might discard the two. What do you then play on the next round of the suit? You have an even number left, which means you should play a high card. What difference would it make if you play count discards? In this case, presumably you must discard the two because at that point you had an odd number left. Although it might appear superficially that *remaining count* simplifies matters, it does complicate positions like these. Like *obvious shift*, *remaining count* lacks its own entry in the 6th edition of *The Official Encyclopedia of Bridge*. This says something about the method's popularity – or lack of it.

If you do not like complications, I suggest you stop reading now. What I am about to discuss is in a different league from the rest of the book.

You must have noticed that one problem with defensive signals is that declarer can tune in and pick up the signals, often gaining as much information as the other defender. The idea with *encrypted signals* is to stop this from happening. The defenders play two different systems, usually depending upon what they hold in a 'key' suit.

The key suit is a suit in which declarer's holding in the suit is known or presumed. For example a 2♠ response to Stayman, especially if the opposing style is not to open 1NT with a decent five-card major, will often mean exactly four spades. When declarer has shown four spades in this way, the defenders will know how many spades each other has as soon as dummy appears. To benefit from this knowledge they might agree that a defender with an even number of spades gives standard count, attitude and suit-preference signals while a defender with an odd number of spades gives reverse signals. Obviously the defenders do not give count signals in the spade suit itself, which means that, until one of them shows out of spades, declarer will not know what type of signals the defenders are giving.

As someone who thinks that the laws of the game are weighted too heavily towards the declarer, I heartily support this type of agreement. Unfortunately, many of the bridge authorities do not see it the same way and you will need to check whether *encrypted signals* are legal in the circles in which you play.

The example I gave above is one of a number of possible keys to use. Another possibility is that the declaring side uses Blackwood and then subsides at the five level. In this case, presumably the defenders have two aces between them. Someone with an even number of aces then gives standard signals and someone holding an odd number gives reverse. A variant these days is if Roman Key-Card Blackwood reveals that one of the defenders holds the trump queen. Whoever has it, gives one type of signal and the other gives the opposite. A further possibility is to use a suit in which declarer shows out early in the play. In those cases, both defenders will know who started with an odd or even number of cards in the suit and can encrypt their signals accordingly.

If you have a creative mind, you will no doubt be able to think of a whole host of other situations in which it is possible to establish a key. Perhaps I can just mention one more. It takes a bit of explaining. All players' hands have either three even suits and one odd suit, or three odd suits and one even. 4-4-3-2, 5-4-2-2, and 7-4-2-0 are all examples of three evens and an odd. 4-3-3-3, 5-4-3-1 and 6-3-3-1 are examples of three odds and an even. You might agree to use one method of signals with three odd suits and another method with three even suits.

I strongly suggest that you become thoroughly familiar with one set of signals before you attempt to use two on the same deal, which you do with *encrypted signals*.